Humanagerie

Edited by

Sarah Doyle
and Allen Ashley

Humanagerie
edited by Sarah Doyle and Allen Ashley
ISBN: 978-1-908125-81-1

First published 2018

www.eibonvalepress.co.uk

Humanagerie

CONTENTS

Animal Apology

Paul Stephenson

Sorry if I fling zoos at you, and when I do,
forelegs spread, the bony tufts of giraffe heads
rip up kitchen tiles, elongations of neck vertebrae
swinging hard and fast like a blotchy orange 5-iron.

You should probably duck when lobbed elephants swirl
through the living room's low-watt sky, Zeppelins deflating,
trunks dangling like loose grey guy-ropes, brushing the blinds.

And about the single-horned rhinos and hippos, yes, I know:
all that stomping, stampeding, at some small thing you say,
the mud-soaked noses, nostrils flaring up like fireplaces,

odd-toed ungulates charging into your hell-of-a-day,
unleashing the fury of a fenced and caged species,
the paying visitors peering and gaping, leaning in
to watch us both, not breeding here in captivity.

Beginnings

Elaine Ewart

A rustle of leaves. I stop by the hedge:
a suspicion of movement. I wait, longing
to peer in at the clotted feathers.

The attraction of starting again,
to break damply from an egg:
to get it right this time.

I can only listen and imagine
the chicks' scraggy bodies'
rapid bulge and deflate. For them,
new is already a lifetime.

Aquarium Dreams

Gary Budgen

Blind Cave Tetras (*Astyanax mexicanus*)

My brother Jason wanted to be a marine biologist but knew, deep down, it wasn't for the likes of us. He was only two years older but he always looked after me. When we heard Dad's fumbled key in the front door Jason would get me up to our room. I would be crying by the time we got there, the shouting downstairs having already started.

"It's all right," he'd say and put his arm around me. "It's all right. Let's go look at the fish."

Inside the fish tank the guppies fluttered their tails and the red blue neon tetras darted in and out of the empty windows of the ruined castle. Jason hadn't really liked it when I bought him that castle. It wasn't natural but he'd put it in there to please me. I think it was probably better than the other things I could have bought, the pirate ship, the diver's helmet or the skull.

None of it was natural really. Jason had explained it to me. These fish would never be together in the wild, they came from different parts of the world. The guppies were from little pools in Trinidad, the neon tetras from Peru. You put them together because they got along, didn't tear at each other's tails with their mouths or butt each other. It was what was called in the hobby a fresh water community tank.

Downstairs as the shouting got louder, as a plate smashed I imagined being inside the aquarium, floating above the perfectly smooth gravel stones, weaving in and out the labyrinths of rock and plant and castle ruins, a fish oblivious to the human world.

"One day," Jason would say, "I'll get a proper marine tank with tangs and Talbot's damsels, dottybacks and firefish. A little piece of ocean."

Then he'd read to me from his favourite book, *Fishes Dangerous to Man*. He'd read to me about sharks and barracudas. Inside the tank I sometimes spotted the blind cave tetras, unlike the beautiful neon tetras these were ugly, with anaemic bodies that revealed hints of their inner organs and only sockets where their eyes should be. After millennia in the dark they'd adapted to do without light.

When the house had gone quiet Mum would come up to our room. Dad would be crashed out on the sofa by then. There would be no bruises or marks, no trace of tears on her face. She would give us her beautiful cracked smile, her eyes lighting up.

"My lovely boys."

We understood we weren't to see what was going on.

As we got older Jason continued with his interest in all things aquatic while my thing was music. Mum got me a guitar from the Freeman's catalogue, an acoustic that had a pick-up so it could be plugged into an amp. I formed a band that really took off when I met Vince who went to Askes Grammar School. None of us usually mixed with Askes kids but Vince was all right. He had a great record collection. He played us lots of blues. He said he was preparing us to hear something that would change us forever. That something was *Trout Mask Replica* by Captain Beefheart.

We were stoned in my bedroom.

"This is what we should sound like," Vince drawled.

Jason was dropping brine shrimp in to the top of the fish tank

"What a racket," he said laughing.

"It's a message from hell," Vince pronounced.

We'd spent a lot of time arguing about what we should call the band. Vince had suggested The Swordfish, after the Tom Waits' album. I wasn't sure. I thought that in the end though Vince would just tell us what were to be called but instead our name was just waiting there for us that day, splashed across the cover of one of Jason's fish magazines, a caption for the eyeless white creatures, The Blind Cave Tetras.

Our first and only gig was at the Newlands Tavern, in the backstreets beyond Nunhead Cemetery. It was one of those pubs you got back then, obscure but on the music circuit. Vince knew someone in a band called The Spiders and they said we could support them if we brought in our own backline.

The gig was fly posted around Peckham and New Cross. Well, not our gig specifically but all the gigs that month at the Newlands. Our name was in a little box beneath The Spiders. You could hardly see it but I didn't care. I tried to tear one of the posters off the wall but it just ripped. I cut the listing out of the NME though.

"You've got to come," I told Jason.

But I knew it wasn't his thing. He would stay at home, reading in front of the fish tank, his thoughts straying occasionally to where I was that night.

Vince was really hyped up but it wasn't the audience he was expecting. A group of ageing Camberwell skinheads had shown up. We managed to get most of the way through one song. I played a basic three chord rhythm and the synth player, who thought he was Brian Eno, twiddled out weird noises. The drum machine kept up a repetitive beat while Vince in black lipstick and eyeliner did his thing as a front man.

We love to watch, tickety-boo.
We love to watch, tickety-boo.
We love to watch.
We love to watch.
We love to watch.

This was repeated, sometimes with the salacious innuendo of a voyeur, sometimes as the sinister midnight confession of an agent in a police state.

There were jeers, shouts of *fucking poof.* Then someone threw a glass and it hit the synth player. The skinheads stormed the stage.

"Blind tetras," a huge bone head said as he tried to punch me and fell short, "How come you like to watch then?"

13

He seemed to think it was the funniest thing anyone had ever said.

The bouncers soon steamed in and broke it all up but the gig was over and we all went back to my house. That night Dad had somehow made it upstairs to his own bed and Mum was with Jason in the kitchen. She made us cups of tea and I told them both what had happened.

Mum laughed, told Vince she liked his make-up and could he give her some tips. For a moment it was as though I was seeing a person I'd never seen before. I could imagine her my own age, lively, a bit of a joker. I wanted to stay in that moment forever.

Blind cave tetras have lateral lines, highly sensitive hairs that link to receptive cells. These can detect fluctuating water pressure. In aquariums the blind cave tetras sense the glass borders of their world, their imprisonment. They dream of their lost cave systems, the flooded tunnels of Mexico because who would want their dreams to be confined to an aquarium?

I never saw Vince again, but heard that he went on to become a DJ, playing in pubs. Other people's music, not his own.

Moon Jellyfish (*Aurelia aurita*)

Jason got a job in the tropical fish shop near Peckham Rye. It's not there nowadays. Like a lot of things. I went to college and the guitar gathered dust, tucked beneath my bed. On Saturdays I would go and see Jason, watching as he wiped clean the glass of the tanks, fed shrimp and flakes to the fishes. There were aisles of tanks with fluorescent lights illuminating the colours of the fish, the rocks and miniature jungles.

One time I went and he was at the back of the shop where there was a tank with jellyfish, their translucent bodies glowing. They hardly had a will of their own, going with the currents made by the mechanical pump.

"You see," Jason said, "it's a covered pump. You can't use a normal aquarium pump for filtering or aeration because the jellyfish would just get sucked it and mangled."

"They sting don't they?" I asked.

"Some jellyfish sting. These ones do, but it's pretty mild. You just have to wear gloves when you clean out the tank. There are worse ones of course. But then on some islands in the Pacific there are lakes that have been cut off from the sea. The jellyfish there have been isolated from predators for so long they have evolved so they don't sting anymore, you can dive there, swim with them."

I was hardly listening to what he was saying, transfixed as I was with the glowing bodies of the jellyfish.

"They're beautiful."

"It's the artificial lighting," Jason said, "These moon jellyfish don't glow naturally. There are some that do like the crystal jellyfish. It's bioluminescent. It glows on its own."

"Wow."

I imagined what it might be like. To float like that, without thought, no brain, no nervous system. A thing made of water trapped between two thin layers of see-through skin. A creature hardly distinct from the sea.

Back at home things were better. Dad had gone, pissed off out one night and not come back. Mum was cleaning offices in the West End mornings and then all evening. She never talked about him. I wanted to believe it was because the very trace of him had gone, that any particle of him that had remained in our environment had been pulled away by unseen currents.

"Where do you think he's gone?" I asked Jason one evening after Mum had gone to work.

I'd been thinking about him. Perhaps he'd returned to me in a dream, a lurking anxiety.

"Don't know. Don't care. Long as he doesn't come back." He went back to reading his book.

Then I saw Dad. It was November and I was coming home from college and he was there, out beyond the smeared window of the bus on a gloomy street. He was stood there smoking in the front of the lit plate glass of a bookies that was closing for the evening.

I tried to ignore it. Go with the flow. Hang around at college with people and get into whatever they were into, the right music, drugs, the right way to look. I didn't want to see what was around me, wanted only to feel the brightness of the moment.

A moon jellyfish knows the world through rhopalia, tiny organs around their body used for sensing light, movement and direction with respect to gravity. Jellyfish do not let anything coalesce into sharp outlines.

I saw him again, another betting shop, closer to home. Another time going into one of his old watering holes round the corner from our house.

Then he came back. The locks had never been changed and he shambled into the kitchen where me and Jason had just finished tea.

"Where is she?" he asked. His foot scuffed against the leg of the table.

"She's at work," said Jason.

"What work?"

"Why don't you just go," I said. "Why don't you just leave us alone?"

He slumped forward, palm on the table. He stank of booze and fags.

"Big man are you now?" he said laughing. It was a laughter no-one else would ever join in with.

"Fuck off," I told him.

He lunged at me then, hands outstretched as though he'd throttle me. I would have probably got out of the way anyway but by then Jason had picked up the nearest kitchen knife and was slicing the air. Dad stepped back and stumbled and fell hitting his head on the cooker. He lay there with a pool of blood forming around his head while we waited for an ambulance to come.

Dad turned out ok. Lots of blood but no real damage. But he always was a vindictive bastard and decided to press charges. Probably all part of some scheme, some game, to get Mum to take him back. Dad embellished his tale. Jason was a violent thug, a menace. Jason would cause more trouble… Back then kids were held before trial if they were thought to be a risk. Jason was put on remand in an adult prison. It shouldn't have happened but it routinely did, people said that to us afterwards, said it was a scandal. When we visited him he looked as though whatever had once given him life had been drained away.

"Dad wants me to go and see him about it all," said Mum.

"Don't see him," said Jason. "I'll be all right."

Who knows what went on in those last days? I don't like to think about it. When I picture his end I see him not dangling from a rope made from a filthy bath towel but rather in an ocean, flowing to and fro within its rhythms. Filled with light.

Bull Shark (*Carcharhinus leucas*)

Outside the newly opened London Aquarium. I would never go inside. I didn't need to. There was more than an aquarium within me. Yet I liked to be near, to be close to those inside. I watched the people. I loved to watch. A fish among the human artefacts, the pirate ships and coral castles.

After Jason, Mum wasn't the same. She hardly went out but instead sat in front of the TV every day. She didn't want to do anything else. Dad disappeared. In my head he was lying on the kitchen floor, blood still pooling. I sniff for him, try to locate him by his blood, iron red, overpowering his booze stink, the tang of it making me hunger. But if he had been bleeding I would have been able to find him because I can smell blood at one part per million.

I would have to search. When I found him I would devour him.

I wandered places I'd heard rumour of him, traces sensed on the currents of the superhighway, electronic impulses of names like his, only they were always dead ends. I went to new towns and looked. I loved to watch. Shopping malls in the hour before they closed. The people moving in a different way then, using the places as a short cut, say, from the railway station to the high street and the residential streets beyond. They hardly glanced in the shop windows but made directly for home or the only places doing business: the supermarket and the late opening chemists. This wasn't an hour for frivolity. I loved to watch. Saturday afternoon, crowds spilling in and out, washing back and forth from high street to mall, from mall to high street. I kept looking.

The world changed. The era of hope, which began with the opening of the London Aquarium and was something even I couldn't ignore, seemed to be coming to a close. I swam among those I thought of as the dead, who would soon all float to the top of the tank. Then one day I saw, on a portable TV high on a kebab shop wall, aeroplanes fly into a building of glass panes. The tank had finally shattered. The fourth wall had been violated forever.

One disaster followed another. Each had to be forgotten in preparation for the next.

A bull shark can survive where it shouldn't, swimming up estuaries, leaving salt water behind, always searching. They have been found in lakes in golf courses after floods, even swimming pools. They know all the good places to find meat, the places of left-overs where animal waste washes out from slaughter houses.

I searched Sally Army hostels, pubs and betting shops. The submarine landscape of the bottom dweller. These were places of detritus but then that is what my father was, while I was sleek, with a streamlined body, missile like, the archetype shark, efficient no-nonsense grey. When I closed my mouth it was a slit made with a Stanley knife, when I opened it there was razor wire.

I thought I would live like this forever but one day I found myself near the old neighbourhood again. The geography had changed. Rotherhithe and Bermondsey were mostly underwater, the river stretched wide to New Cross where the land began to rise to form the new shore line. Apparently the Thames Barrier had been destroyed in a terrorist attack and London had become a city of water. It was as though I had imposed my vision onto the outer world.

I slept on a bench in Pepys Park. It wasn't cold, the weather rarely got cold now. In the morning the parakeets fluttered about, the pond was full of sticklebacks that almost lured me in.

All that day I searched. I went, as I had so long ago, to the places where he had used to go. Some of them were now in the flood zone but there was still The Ship, The Gold Diggers Arms and The White Horse. I wandered through places I used to know, past shops boarded up or covered in metal grilles, whole zones of burnt out houses where there had been riots.

It was evening when I found him. The Anchor. Men stood at the bar, staring down into pints, others were at tables on their own. There was hardly any talk, there was no music. In this silence, in this stillness I circled, pretending indifference, all the while my senses stretched out, felt the vibrations as he picked up his pint then put it down again, as he fingered lovingly the shot glass next to it. I felt the disturbance of his muscles, the rise and fall of his chest as he breathed. I circled and made my way to the other end of the bar hardly looking at him.

When I moved in it would all be over quickly. I would circle and bump the prey, then close and bite. I'd keep biting until he was incapable of anything but death.

He didn't notice me he was so intent on his drinking, then calling the barman over for more. Hardly a word passed between them, no conviviality. When the barman came over to me, perched now on a bar stool, he took my order silently. I stared over at Dad and saw him properly for the first time.

There was a bandage around one hand. He must have been bleeding again, drawing me to him after all this time. His skin was bleached out, scored with crevices. His hair was matted, sticking up in odd places in tufts. He wore a shabby jacket that was stained with food. He was broken and old. I wondered how I could ever have been afraid of him.

I left the pub, my drink untouched.

When I arrived home Mum was where she always was, sat on the sofa watching the TV.

"So you're back," she said, "Everyone seems to be going back to where they started now the end is coming."

19

As soon as she said this I realised the simple truth of it. I shrugged.

"What you been doing with yourself?" she asked.

"I was a shark," I said.

"What?"

"I was a shark but I don't think I am now."

I went upstairs to the old room. It was exactly as I'd left it. Jason's stuff was still there. A thin layer of dust covered the beds, the shelves, the carpet. The guitar was there beneath my bed. The aquarium stood where it always had. At some point it had been emptied of water but all the fixtures were there, the castle, the gravel and rocks, the plastic plants. The pump had fallen from the side where its sucker had dried out. Everything stank and lay in ruins. It was as beautiful as a beach covered in the splinters of a fabulous ship wreck. Soon I would walk out onto that beach, I would breathe, I would watch, I would wait for the sea to come in and claim me.

Beetle

Sarah Westcott

Solace drove me to this place,
its green hollows,
searching again for your form, love,
for it has been seven years –
billy-witch, bewitcher, solstice creeper,
bold-blinded beast.

I went to the road, its ranks of shimmering carmine,
looking for you at the edges of belief –
you, a Da Vinci sketch
testing the limits of flight
ahead of your time
or back with the dinosaur brutes,
out of this world of nets and cables and glare.

I longed for you to cross my palm,
scarab – smooth as a knee cap,
complicated as a music box
held together with tiny pinions,
the intricate pins and tucks
of your mechanics
working the unforgiving air –

I took you apart in my mind, found nothing
but a mandible like a wishbone,
one serrated, iconic antler
of bravado, lost bravado.
I keep it for my rising son,
our last mid-summer walks,
his tender voice breaking in the dusk.

Note
*The larvae of the stag beetle (which is becoming increasingly rare) live in
the soil for seven years before emerging as fully-grown adults.*

Vixen

Cheryl Pearson

I light for the den of hindleggers.
The all-on-ups who flummox and fuss
at our slinkings-in. Keepers of cluckers
who make good our bellies, whose blood
beaters patter like rain under feathers.

I follow my teeth to the red-to-come,
follow my own gold lights over grass.

Oh, bloodsmell! Oh, flush of rust! A flood
to loosen, a feast of salt when I open.

Quickquick I go, a lick of heat in the garden,
then gone. Six yellow eyes in the den-mouth
blinking off and on. *Mother,* and *hunger,*
the words are the same. I dance with risk
on black toes, fill the coops with snow.

I'd rob the world of bones to feed these
flames. Flicker, children. Flicker now.

Augury

Tarquin Landseer

With his patter flash
he chatters the jargon of thieves.
Snazzy in his parti-coat
of teal glancing light,
he'll jazz up the street
with a hopscotch on paving
as five band round a fur bag
to clack over a maggot-pie.

From a chequered past
pied snatch-purse
is a curse of a yackety bird
that wags a wand of tail
ready with a jinx.
Spit thrice at the risk
of being absurd
or he'll steal your run of luck.

Doyen of the crows
with a *chacker chacker*
that can't be sung;
a drop of devil's blood
under the wagging tongue.
Pica pica craves coins;
gold trinkets catch the eye.
A diet of oddities
that asks a wonder why.

Otherwise
he stashes his secrets
never to be sold,
joins a requiem of birds;
observes obsequies
after the crack of death,
then fashions a wreath
with tufts of grass and moss
in sorrow
and was always
stationed at each cross.

The Orbits of Gods

Holly Heisey

I. Outer Circle

We orbit him because he is our god. His scent is authority, his mind sharp as rock-honed teeth. His fur gleams black like the void and eyes shine red with bloodlust, as they should. This is what the inner circle tells us. He commands through them, they who share some of his godness. One day, we will be them.

II. Inner Circle

The outer circle is rabid. They growl and snap at us to show regard for our strength, paws churning up dust, but they only wish to gain our ranks. Our god knows we are better than them. We take polite nips at him. We howl in agreement with his proclamations. We will, at some point, become equals.

III. God

They think I am their god. They don't know what I have done. My scent is full of death, and they call it perfume.

IV.   God Before

My brood brother ran the edge of the outer circle – lean muscle, mottled pelt, tight sinew. I planned to puncture his throat deep enough to weaken him, to show that I, the youngest of our brood, was stronger. That I could get in the outer circle and orbit our god. But my brother fought with all his strength, hard claws scraping rough gravel, fangs tearing at my skin and fur, throat vibrating with his fury. I bled and I tasted his blood, rich with a power I craved. I lunged and tore his belly open. His belly, which he'd never bared to me willingly.

There is a moment when you have killed a brother where you feel, in the span of one breath: the triumph over a better; the sinking of a heart; the taste of your own blood power; a premonition of the numbness that will grow.

V.   God in the Outer Circle

I spent two seasons of the sun in the outer circle. They respected me for how I had achieved the orbit of my god, yet I was one of many who had come there by blood.

A female in the outer circle found my scent agreeable. Together we chased the others, snapping at the inner circle. Yipping and howling our taunts, our bodies taut, our fangs bared. Often, we came close to breaking into their ranks. At night we rested under the stars – I would lay my head on the soft fur of her neck, and later she would rest her head on mine. We ate the scraps filtered down from what the birds flew to our god. We were of one soul.

✳

27

VI.   God in the Inner Circle

One day, we parted a path into the inner circle, and they could do nothing but let us stay. One of their number fell to the outer circle and was churned out as unworthy of orbiting our god. It was the way of things.

My mate and I learned to nip more gently, with finesse. We learned how in the inner circle, every movement meant eight different things. We danced, weaving our bodies in cooperation and competition.

We learned not to fear our god.

VII.   Fall of a God

My mate and I were unstoppable. We were the best of the inner circle. We had three pups, gray and black and mottled, which were carried with reverence out of orbit. They would grow and learn to hunt. They would bring meat in their jowls to the birds that flew to our god, who would bestow meat to the inner circle, who would filter the dregs to the outer circle, who would toss the scraps to the unworthy.

My mate and I saw our god. His fur was shaggy and did not gleam so black, and his muscles had gone to fat from gorging himself on meat. His eyes were golden, not red, and weary.

We were stronger than he. We attacked, and he fell.

VIII.   The Orbits of Gods

Our ancestors came from the stars. I learned the stories as a pup; each star in the sky was like one of our gods. Each had an inner circle on a world that was warm and bright, and an outer circle on cooler worlds who fought for the rights to the inner circle. Outside, the unworthy would barely feel the pull of their god-star, and never its warmth.

Two gods cannot exist in the same place. My mate and I toppled a god and became gods ourselves, but we could no longer stay mates. We burned so bright, our teeth so sharp, that we would have killed each other.

We howled at our loss. We had not known. We had thought it would be different for us, we could rule together. But two stars cannot burn in the same place in the same sky.

We are gods, but different stars. Our circles orbit us; our birds bring us meat. I whisper through the birds messages to my mate. *I love you. I am sorry it ended this way.* She fears for our children; we don't want them to go into orbit around us. There are other paths, even if they are seen as unworthy.

There is nothing more unworthy than to be a god.

I now understand why our god let us kill him. He could never have killed me, his son.

Polymorphous / Stages of Growth

Olivia Edwards

Stage 1. Soft flesh / small hands
      You were hatched into this world, not birthed
      And from a shattered shell you rose
      Scale to skin as hands to fins
Stage 2. Webbed feet / house trained
      They didn't notice it at first
      You were perfect for so long
      But something changed
Stage 3. Cold blood / migratory
      You were left fatherless and your mother
      Well, she didn't understand
      You were never venomous
Stage 4. Feral / winged
      It wasn't hard, saying goodbye

Pray

Scott Hughes

Look, here in my palm as this praying mantis
turns its pyramid head. Keep your mouth
closed. It will count your teeth, and if it finishes,

you will die. Watch its legs, tapered to points.
Watch its spiny arms like broken tusks fold in prayer,
worshipping the chitinous god of stained-glass wings,

of exoskeletons, of antennae sensual as tongues
or fingertips. I raise it to my face to see if it will count
my teeth, numbering each one with its pointed spur.

I see my face captured in the inky dome of its eye.
Does it understand its own head mirrored in my pupil
as its forelegs conduct an arthropodal choir I cannot hear?

Seahorse

Tarquin Landseer

In the serene shallows
behind a greenery of sea grass,
two of a kind
fan each other with a blur of fins.
By the moon-glade,
while shoals reel in a gyre,
they nod their bony heads
before the rarefied dance
above a stretch of meadow
thinned out.

For all his worth
he thrusts a herd of foals
from the brood pouch;
scatters them like question marks,
the time ahead in doubt.

Sun-dried marine curios,
placebos for the rheumy-eyed;
a dusty answer lies
inside a pill sold to spur a growth.

Little chimeras of wild fancy
in the false light of aquaria
hang like mementos;
or equine as knight figurines
set in resin,
still with armorial bearings
in a miniature *tableau vivant.*
Hollow keepsakes kept
as tokens of remembrance.

Crow and Rat

James Dorr

His name was Crow, and she was called Rat. Both were beggars in the New City, not the creative kind, *jongleurs* or tale-tellers, gossip-mongers or criers or news-spreaders, but rather the shabbier, desperate grubbers of others' detritus – ghouls as it were of the wealthier precincts' trashheaps and middens. Petty thieves, sometimes, when courage and opportunity blessed them. In other words, common enough to be unnoticed.

Rat, in particular, lived in the sewers, a place forbidden and dangerous. Many a time she battled huge lizards, kin to the crocodiles known by the ancients, or vied with great underground spiders for the rights to a passageway opening, perhaps, on the river. Or possibly inland, beneath some park where the wealthier congregated at nightfall, perhaps to attend to an entertainment and thus unmindful of slender hands and arms reaching upward through some loose grating, to clutch at purses or low-hanging jeweled pendants.

Things that could be, were sold on subsequent evenings in parts of New City unknown to polite folk, where stores existed that bought such items. Questions as to their provenance unasked. The days between were spent under the ground, safe from the burning rays of a sun grown ever hotter over the years until even the rich could not go out by daylight unless protected by hats and thick, all-encompassing *chadors*.

It was in such a shop that she met Crow. Or, rather, she saw him, as if from afar, for even among beggars there were some degrees of rank. Crow, in his feather-suit, among the higher, he a thief who would swoop down from ledges often mere moments before a new dawn, when even the wealthiest must scurry homeward, unwatchful and flustered, mindful only of reaching shelter before the sun's rising.

Easy prey for Crow, black-masked and black-suited, loose folds outstretched as if wings to help guide him down. Razors attached to his boots like talons – a stoop and a grab, a pool of blood left behind. But rarely killing, especially if such a victim's companions could rally about him, helping him to his feet, acting as guides if need be for the final few blocks to his home. The commotion caused, of course, helping Crow to escape, mask possibly reversed, razors retracted, feathers turned inward, covered with mufti. Indeed, it was said sometimes that Crow even helped, if a man had no friends with him, often gaining entrance to victims' homes that way. Helping them to their beds. Using the day then to loot at leisure, making his getaway first thing the next night.

Rat sighed. She had heard of Crow – rumors abounded. Some said that he could actually fly!

Others said, no, that he was a charlatan, just like everyone else of their station. A gentleman, yes, perhaps, higher than most of the class of beggars but he could afford it. As often *they* could not.

And still, others said, he had no woman. No fair companion to help him and love him.

His eyes fell on Rat, sinuous and dark-haired, almost a river princess in her sleekness but, in her case, more adapted for slithering through pipes and joints, through tunnels and dark places. She, too, occasionally entered homes in the wealthier districts, emerging from drains that, perhaps, had been opened for repairs, their inward-curving spikes no longer guarding the riches that lay above, waiting to be plucked like flowers from a tree. Pulled down, that way, after her.

Slender and slick, her skin a dead, pasty white, her eyes met his too; hers red, almost, his dark and beaded.

"Excuse me," he said as he shoved his way past her. "Milady," he added.

She curtsied. "My pleasure," she said – she had been taught that much by her mother, now long since deceased. She still remembered with horror the ghouls' work three days after when her mother's corpse had been brought to them, dumped over the borderline into Old City, because no one had had the means to see it buried. She, for her part, vowed the ghouls would not have *her*, when her time came too. Better to stay in the sewers where she lived, to let real rats devour her.

"My pleasure," she said again. "You are the one called Crow?"

But he had gone. He had already disappeared, his feathers turned inward, to blend in blackness into the nighttime crowd.

So life went on among those called the dregs of the beggars of New City. Rat had gained a small measure of notice, because, so the gossip said, Crow spoke to *no one*. But he had talked to Rat, even excusing himself in his hurry. Even addressing her as his *lady*.

It was still a small thing, Rat tried to convince herself. He'd murmured something, even the taciturn sometimes did *that* when manners required it. Even among beggars. And he'd said "Milady", not knowing her name.

And yet it was more. Her heart told her that much, pounding and fluttering whenever she thought of that moment, now weeks past. Whenever she heard a rumor come back to her, exaggerated of course with retelling as rumors are wont to be. That he had said not "Milady," but "My love." That he had not just brushed against her, but *kissed* her. And possibly more too, until only she knew the truth of the matter. And she knew one thing more, that even in that encounter of moments, their eyes had met, sparking and dangerous. And that she loved *him*.

As the months went by after, she followed his exploits, through rumors and broadsides. She never saw him again, except in crude pictures, but she attempted to see in her mind what his life must be like. And while she stuck to her own home and habits, she tried in her way to imitate what she saw. Increasing her boldness. No longer, for instance, shrinking from spiders except when she *must* fight, but now on occasion seeking them out herself. Killing and eating them.

This too was noised about in New City among the least well placed of its beggars. This too was grist for the mills of rumorers, no doubt exaggerated, too, in its way. Nevertheless at base with some truth to it.

Her skin did take a healthier sheen, her hair more lustre. Some saw in her beauty – perhaps she was worthy of one such as Crow. This the rumors said also.

Rat was realistic. She dared not even hope, not when awake at least.

But in her dreams, ah! Perhaps that was different. Perhaps in her dreams – perhaps even in *his* too – black feathers enfolded the white skin of thighs and breasts. His beaked mask removed, perhaps red lips met those redder.

Rat would awake shivering, yet overly warm as well. Sometimes she even feared that she might be ill, but, as she plied her work, she felt her senses to be, if anything, more acute. Not less. Her body to be stronger. Not showing weakness.

Her life was improving, if only because she had something to reach for. A thing she would not get – she was still a realist. But she could still aspire. All the time still seeking gossip of Crow's exploits, hearing almost every few weeks of some new adventure, bolder and more outrageous than those before. Sometimes hearing as well rumors of *herself,* some deed she had done but as others saw it – these growing more noticed too.

It was a strange feeling, happy yet sad also. Exhilarating, yet fearful as well. As she would wake, trembling yet anticipating. A new night's escapade set out before her, for success or failure. It may not have mattered.

It was not the deed for her – the love was enough. Never mind hope for its consummation.

So it was for Rat the night Crow was killed. He who the rumors said even could *fly*. However, when she came to see him, hearing the gossip, she found his body broken and alone, struck down by some disease of the sort that were rife in the New City's seedier neighborhoods.

"Who has come for him?" she asked the city guardians who found him.

"None, milady," the first one said. The second one added, "Are you the one they call Rat?"

She nodded. "Yes."

"Then you must take him. From what we have heard, he had no other friends. No one else who loved him."

She nodded again. And now she had his corpse, the things that were with it. His feather-suit and mask. His purse, empty, which did not surprise her as *others* had found him first. To the point, *she* had no money either.

She thought of her mother, the ghouls, her vow, as she dragged him into the nearest sewer. This was a cross-pipe that led to the better residential precincts – she knew these pipes like the back of her hand. If she took another outlet to her right, she would come to the New City Government District. Its tallest buildings.

She lifted his body, surprised by its lightness, a legacy of the illness that killed him. A plan was beginning to form in her mind.

She would *not* let it be eaten by ghouls, nor by sewer rats either. She carried it in her arms, taking the right fork, until she was under a building she knew. *La Tour du Maire* – the Mayor's Tower. There she put it down and rested.

She was attacked once – a marauding centipede which she killed quickly, twisting its head from its thrashing body, avoiding its venomous fangs. Now she was angry – *this* was what it came to, that she might have Crow only when he was dead? Then she would do well by him, taking his corpse to the Tombs itself, the vast necropolis across the river where those more fortunate than her kind were interred. She was an expert at breaking into places where she was not wanted, as Crow had been also.

And why not the Tombs then? But not by the causeway where dead were delivered on the groaning corpse-carts that plied their way every night, flush with donations to pay for their passage. Nor skulking by day, as some poor people did, to leave their deceased by the charity gate in the hope they might thus gain a pauper's shallow hole.

No. Crow in his prime had been larger than life. And so, in her way, had she become also, at least among the lowest of the low. And thus, for both their sakes, she would at least try –

She lifted his corpse again, this time stripping it, placing its feather-suit on her own body. She studied the suit's secrets, finding out how it worked. How its wings stiffened with strong, telescoping wires, letting one glide, if not actually fly. Putting its boots on, trying out not just retractable razors, but strange, suction-cup devices on their soles, tubes to run up her legs, bulbs to control them; its similar gloves, its grapples and climbing hooks.

Trying his mask on.

The next night she stole a rope, down by the river, coiled on a boat near an overflow outlet. Braving the stench of the river's poisons.

She paused for a moment to gaze at the Tombs, its lights glowing green on the river's far side, engendered by luminescent fungi, and then to turn to the New City behind her with its harsher, brighter, neon yellows and blues and purples, oranges and maroons. Seeing, above all, its highest tower: *La Tour du Maire.*

The third night she lashed Crow's corpse to her own body, front to front, to leave her winged back free. She emerged from the sewer into an alley, and started her climb up the great building's side.

At the tenth or twelfth story she came to a ledge, surmounted by gargoyles and projecting sills, the latter just high enough for her to creep under, Crow still roped to her breast. There she rested, avoiding the sun's rays as dawn became full day, until the next night.

This time she climbed with Crow twenty further floors up, getting increasingly used to the suit's secret features, and on the night following, thirty or more – who could count them all? – until, before she knew it, she had reached the summit.

It was again almost dawn, but this time there was nothing higher in all of New City around her for her to hide under. She was in Crow's lair now! She gazed about her, standing at her full height, at the blue ghoul lights to the south and far west, the great river continuing in darkness to north, the first glowing cloud tops to east and south where the sun would soon rise in its deadly splendor, and, at last, again to west, nearer this time, to the river and, past it, across the causeway still dotted with lights from the last of the corpse trains. The wall and its great gate, its portcullis closing. And, beyond, the Tombs with its central, stepped pyramid where it was said an Emperor was buried, the angel statue that marked its top. The angel looked toward the New

City, but upward as well, as if its eyes sought to meet hers, as Crow's eyes had on that night so long past.

But she had Crow now, and his feather-suit too. She tightened the lashings that held his corpse to her, kissing it once on its dead, yet warming lips, then pressed the buttons extending her wings' wires. Feeling the wind that rustled her feathers, catching the whiff of a rising, dawn fog, she launched herself forward.

For a moment, she actually flew. She had not been able to practise, of course, with the suit in the air before, but she had innately a sense of balance. Had she been prettier she might have been able to live as a dancer. But as it was, she felt the ways of the wind, its gusts and its swirlings. The minute corrections the suit's wingtips needed. And, gliding to west, she actually flew!

But then it was over. The suit, after all, had been made for one person – as light as it was from the sickness that struck him down, the added burden of Crow's body tied to Rat's strained the suit's wings too much. First, with a *crack*, the right wing folded, the wires that stiffened it shattering in pieces. Rat and Crow spinning. And then the left, too, leaving only the fabric that flapped between Rat's outstretched arms and her torso to hold them aloft. To act as a glider's wings, although not sufficient to take them beyond the river's center.

She fell with a great splash, a shower of feathers loosed by the impact, caught in the wind sprinkling over the Tombs' wall – that much at least reached their destination. But for Rat and Crow themselves there was just darkness as the river's waters covered them over, poisoning Rat instantly. Acids and wastes already accelerating Crow's own body's deterioration.

Then there was silence, except in the Tombs where a gate guard had seen Crow and Rat as she'd readied herself to launch. Fearing some ghouls' trick, perhaps to seize the newly delivered dead, taking by surprise what strength might not gain for them, he had summoned the guard captain. This one in turn called a curator to him, who made notes and sketches as Rat's and Crow's flight played out.

Then the next night the curator asked the corpse-train drivers in turn what gossip *they* might have heard that might explain it.

And so, in time, he had gathered the story's wisps and pieces together into the tale of Crow and Rat, as it is written here. He had a copy etched on metal and buried with the few of the wings' feathers that actually drifted across the Tombs' wall, and he had a stone carved with a picture of the two, taken from the best of his sketches combined with descriptions from some of the guards, as they struck the river, and he had it mounted above those few remnants.

There it stands to this day.

Phasianus Colchicus

Kerry Darbishire

It's Sunday which means nothing
except high on the fell I know
you're strutting bracken and gorse,
setting fire to the ghyll.

The reach between us closes in
the same early hour when I hear
your double-shriek and shiver enter
my garden. I dream your musk,

your tail feathers burning my skin,
your cool droplets of rain beading
my neck like fresh-water pearls,
as if ancient beauty is all we need.

And Then I Was a Sheep

Jonathan Edwards

and really, what a treat to find myself
among these friend-shaped clouds or cloud-shaped friends
who breathe, who bleat, these lovely bits of meat
on legs, who take me as something to smell

and imitate. How nice it was to wake
and sing myself, to flounce and fling myself
down hillsides someone turned to trampolines
quite suddenly. While others keep their snouts

steadfastly to the ground I blink, I count
my gifts: this four-wheel drive and this cuisine
that grows, the way that I can sigh and mean
that nature is my playground, baby. True,

the farmer, shearing, has looked into my eyes
a little longer than I'd like, as if
he's sussed, he's twigged, and yes, the sheepdog nips
more keenly at my ankles than the others',

but on the whole, I've found, it's easy really
to blend right in, to not stand out. Sometimes,
I miss the feel of the settee beneath me,
a glass of something good, but all in all

I wouldn't go back if I could. I'm less
lonely than I was when I was human,
the world's less cold, now that my winter coat
is part of me, and what I really like

are moonlit nights: us lot, the whole, the flock,
how we all cwtch together in this field,
one living mass of white, one fluffy cloud,
the awesome power of our communal brains –

as if we'd turned the field into the sky,
like we could think it now, and it would rain.

Welsh   English
cwtch   *cuddle or hug*

Wade

Tonya Walter

The truck bobbed along the red dirt road, bouncing in and out of rain-carved trenches and tossing Bee's groceries to the floorboard. The house was only three miles off the main road, but the cautious rolling over rugged terrain took over half an hour. Bee rested her hands on the steering wheel, guiding it from time to time, but for the most part letting the truck sail itself. She rounded the last turn and there, hiding in a cluster of oak trees, was the weathered shack that was her new home.

She'd had no love for her father while he was alive. One summer, when her mother's drinking had taken their car to the beach and left it there half submerged in water, she'd been sent to her father's house in East Texas. He greeted her with a handshake, gave her a tour of his home, which had more rooms than she could imagine uses for, and told her he would be in Europe for the next two months on business. At the summer's end, he sent her a plane ticket and a taxi to the airport.

That had been the whole of her relationship with her father, until the papers had come in the mail.

She had pinned them to her bedroom wall, staring at them while she sipped her morning coffee. Once or twice she even woke in the middle of the night to make sure they were still there, flapping like a large, notarized moth in the breeze of the oscillating fan.

What the papers said in complicated, litigious prose was that her father had died and, in his last days, had decided to will to her, his estranged offspring, a plot of land on the opposite side of the country. The current market value for such a sizeable piece of property was somewhere above $300,000. All she had to do was sign on the dotted line and the lawyers would happily send her a check for the value.

It had been a Whine and Cheese night, when she'd decided to leave. Whenever her roommate Devin survived some small personal crisis, he rewarded himself with cheap red wine and Cheez-its. She would drink and nod along to his rants about rude customers and his casual bomb threats toward his cell phone service provider. On this night, when his impotent rage had burned itself out, he filled his mouth with merlot and took out his cigarettes.

"I don't know how much longer I can stand it here, Bee. Delaware is slowly killing me." He beat the pack against the palm of his hand, shaking his greasy head. "I only stay here for you, you know. I mean, what would you do without me?"

After her mother's death she'd lived alone for one week and it had been terrible. Her imagination was far too active to be left to its own devices. She could feel the weight of silence in every room, bearing down on her like malevolent gravity. To escape the solitude, she had picked up extra shifts at the restaurant. She and Devin had stepped out back for a smoke one evening and she'd listened to his roommate woes for about two minutes before blurting out, "Come live at my place!"

"The real question is, what are *you* going to do without *me*?" She pulled the cork from the bottle, filling her glass almost to the top.

"Oh, you know, eat food out of cans. I'll wear dirty socks all the time and cry myself to sleep at night." He absently searched his pockets for a lighter as he asked, "Are you seriously going for it? You're really loading up the covered wagon and heading West?"

"Maybe," she mused into her wine. "I'd be living rent free. I won't have to listen to the neighbors scream at each other every Friday night. I can sleep and paint and drink. Maybe I'll grow my own vegetables."

"Yeah!" he laughed, "didn't you just kill a Chia pet?"

She threw the cork at his forehead, and he caught it as it bounced off his broad face.

"You could buy a cow! Churn your own butter," he went on, putting his feet up on the pressed wood coffee table, "a regular Laura Ingalls Wilder. Shit, you're going to have trouble fording the rivers by yourself on the way out there. Not to mention all the dysentery."

"I'll stock up on penicillin and water wings."

"Bee, all joking aside," he moved down to the floor and took one of her hands. Looking into her eyes, his voice soft and sincere, he said, "You'll be eaten by snakes."

"Uncle" Pete, one of her mom's old drinking buddies, had gifted her everything an 1850's gold prospector would need: rusted pick-axes, shovels, a weathered post-hole digger. As ridiculous as Pete's well-intentioned gifts had seemed at the time, she was glad to have her antique survival kit.

She hadn't even made it into the cabin that first day before using one of the shovels. A four-foot rattle snake lay stretched over the threshold, an unwelcome mat warding off any would-be visitors.

Looking up into the dusty window of her new home, she imagined the floor inside pulsing with sensuous, reptilian writhing. The light would reflect from their glassy eyes, a deafening orchestra of dry rattles rising from the ground. In her mind, Devin's voice, as textured and real as though he were standing beside her said, "Bee, you'll be eaten by snakes."

One deep breath, and the shovel dropped.

She named it Marie Antoinette and buried it behind the house. That was the beginning of the mass grave of snakes. It was the size of them that horrified Bee. Their bodies were as long as her legs, and the largest of them had sported a head bigger than Bee's fist. Whenever she ventured away from the house, she brought her designated killing spade and made sure it was always within reach.

❋

She gathered the stray grocery items that had rolled onto the passenger side floorboard. There was no electricity in the shanty, and if she wanted a warm meal she had to cook it over a fire. She'd done this twice since moving in, but the California summer had left everything so dry that roasting hot dogs over an open flame felt like barbecuing on a powder keg, or her mother smoking at the gas pumps on those not-quite-sober mornings when Bee was running late to school.

Her small face would watch from the back seat as the numbers flickered and rolled on the pump's small screen, her mom leaning on the trunk with a Virginia Slim pressed between her lips. Bee would close her eyes, feeling her heart race and waiting for the flaming death she was certain would come exploding from that gaping automotive mouth hole, turning the Buick into some fire breathing death machine. But they didn't die. Her hot dog dinners didn't turn the California country side into a blazing inferno either. Bee knew she worried too much, but she still stocked up on ready-to-eat food, avoiding fire as much as possible.

Bee's pants were stained from the knees down with rust red dirt. She'd been working on the driveway for weeks, digging holes and filling holes and rolling the truck up and down the same stretch of road. She could see the progress and, as slow as it was going, felt a satisfaction she had never known before. Her job was simple, and her goal was clear. Life had never been so straight forward.

She could feel the day's work in her shoulders, her body crying out for something more than almonds and granola. Driving back to "the Den," as she had begun to call her ramshackle cabin, she realized that she would gladly risk setting the whole state on fire for one hot meal.

In the old rock ring near the house, she waited for the flames to die down enough to heat her canned beans and ramen noodles, silently chastising herself for not picking up some multivitamins. Something bad was bound to happen if she went too long without eating a vegetable. Her mother had always threatened her with scurvy if she didn't eat her peas.

Her mother hadn't been perfect, but she had tried. Bee's childhood had been a circus. She was never sure if the rides were safe, if the seatbelts were going to hold, if the wheels were going to stay on the tracks. She had survived though, with her mother beside her laughing and teasing Bee for worrying too much. Her mother, who applied mascara while driving down the freeway, steering with one knee and telling Bee to "chill out."

Bee thought her mother would be proud of her now, venturing out into the great unknown. She looked up from the fire to watch the sky bleed color. Neon pinks and orange burned behind purple clouds. The colors were reflected on the surface of the small pond below. The pond was too round to be natural. Someone, long ago, had carved it out of the ground, maybe for swimming, or to stock with fish. Bee watched the liquid sky ripple with the breeze.

One carefree summer her mother had taken her camping. For a month. She said she wanted to "get in touch with nature." Of course, there had been trips to town for booze and hot showers and cigarettes and fast food, but there was lots of nature too. She had tried to drag Bee into the lake one night, but Bee was afraid of the dark water and had dug her heels into the mud. Her mother had laughed, leaving her on the shore and floating off like a crazed water nymph, singing some old hymnal to the stars.

Bee watched the flames and hummed, trying desperately to remember the words of her mother's song as her eyes were drawn again to the pond. Finally, as though accepting a dare, she stood and headed down the hill to the water. She allowed herself only one wary glance back at the fire.

"No worries," she muttered to herself, stripping her clothes as she went, peeling dirty jeans from her legs and leaving them strewn over the ground. She didn't let herself think, but walked to the end of the short pier and jumped in feet first.

The pond was deeper than she had expected. She let herself sink, trying to find the bottom. The water was cool, and she drifted away from the glow of the sky above. Hair floated around her face, dancing gracefully, happily defying the gravity that was always holding it down. She sank deeper, letting bubbles escape past her lips and warble toward the surface. The song in her head played in a loop, and words began to emerge from the tune.

"Wade in the water
Wade in the water children…"

Bee closed her eyes, finally weightless. Something soft drifted around her ankle. Her eyes sprang open, her muscles tensed. Thin tendrils wound around her arms and legs, caressing the back of her neck, groping her face.

Bee panicked, thrashing her limbs, convinced for a moment that the snakes had filled a mass grave of their own. She searched the murky haze, waiting for the curtain of human hair to part and expose a bloated face, eyes clouded and flesh veined, the split skin of gray lips bobbing toward her, begging for a kiss.

The ceiling of water was too far away. Her lungs began to burn as the pond pulled her deeper, away from the air. Bee kicked hard. The water invaded her nose and her throat pulsed in a desperate plea for breath. No one would ever find her down here. No one would even come looking. She would be here for ever, with the swollen, watery dead.

A scream pierced her mind, and Bee realized it was her own as she broke through the surface. After the silence of the pond, her splashes sounded like explosions. She thrashed until she reached shallow water and her feet found muddy earth. Water still blurred her vision as she scrambled blindly toward the fire, tripping over her own abandoned pants and falling to the ground, her fingers clawing at the wet, hairy web that still clung to her face and legs. She scraped handfuls of it from her skin. Spitting the taste of the pond out of her mouth and forcing sprays of water from her nose, she realized, finally, that she had not been attacked by hairy pond zombies. They were just weeds. She'd been caught in a mess of lake weeds.

There was not another human being for miles and still the hot blood of embarrassment filled her face. The light show in the sky was melting down toward the horizon. All shadows were gone. This was the hour of the snake, when the heat of the day receded enough to let them roam free. Bee spat again, forcing her legs into her pants and keeping a sharp eye on the ground as she collected her shirt and hurried back to the campfire.

Of all the things she left behind, she missed warm showers most. There was no way to heat the water and her showers were joyless exercises in efficiency, scrubbing as much of the clay soil from her skin as she could before the cold became too much to bear. Wrapped in her stiff, line dried towel, she watched the muddy cloud at her feet orbit the drain before being sucked into the abyss. Tonight the cold ran bone deep, and her skin tingled with the chill. Summer still ruled the day, but Autumn had begun to claim the nights.

She dressed in her baggy night clothes and grabbed a bottle of water, wishing it was warm tea. She grabbed a fleece throw blanket from the nest of bedding on the floor and sat in the open doorway, watching the moon rise.

Over the cold remains of the fire, Bee caught a flash of a lightning bug. She held her breath, staring and waiting for the green glow to show itself again. She hadn't seen a firefly since leaving Delaware and had assumed their season was over. She closed her heavy eyes, childhood memories bringing a smile to her lips. She had always chased them but never caught them. It wasn't that the bugs got away from her, but that when she found herself close enough to grab them, she always backed away. She was afraid she would break them.

Bee forced her eyes open. The green glow was there, but it didn't flicker like a firefly. Its glow was steady, too still to be any kind of bug. She slid her shoulders up against the door frame, coming to her feet. she felt like the hovering light was watching her. She wrapped the fleece tighter around herself. A loud rush of air, like the sigh of a horse, came from the small green orb. Bee jumped, stumbled sideways into the small house and slammed the door.

Bee woke covered in sweat, tangled in sheets and blankets and sticky hair. Her shoulders and neck had set up like concrete, and her eyes felt like they were on fire. She didn't need a thermometer to tell her she was running a fever. She dragged one leg at a time over to the counter and opened another bottle of water. She only had one more six pack and hoped this was just a 24-hour bug. The thought of bouncing her truck all the way into town made her stomach roll. She searched the small cupboard in the kitchen for her bottle of Ibuprofen.

Outside, the crickets screamed. She couldn't tell how long she'd been asleep. Her bare feet carried her to the fire pit where she took a seat on her stump, savoring the cool air against her face.

"Those crickets..." she thought, distantly. Every hair on her body stood at attention as Bee sensed some nameless threat. She twisted at the waist, holding her stiff neck and looking around at the tangles of scrub oak.

"Those crickets..." she thought again.

The realization crept in slowly. Those crickets weren't crickets. Those crickets were snakes.

She couldn't see any snakes. What she could see was her killing spade propped against the side of the Den, too far for comfort. She rose slowly, so slowly her muscles ached from her near static pose. Her knees wobbled, and it took every ounce of self-control not to make a mad dash to the house. The rattles sounded incredibly close and seemed to be coming from every direction at once.

"No sudden moves," she whispered.

Sidestepping in slow motion, she made her way to the shovel, grabbing it and shuffling slowly toward the corner of the house. Sweat rolled into her eyes, and she wiped it away with her forearm. It could have been from fear or fever, she couldn't tell. She leaned around the corner, squinting into the rapidly dimming light, searching for any movement.

Silence.

The sudden quiet felt like pressure in her ears. Bee stared into shadows, studying each stick on the ground. She hit the shovel against the side of the house, hoping the noise would provoke the snake into giving itself away.

"Thunk, thunk, thunk …thunk …"

The banging of the shovel slowed, then stopped. Beneath her feet, where the bald earth covered the mass grave of snakes, the ground pulsed. Bee blinked, trying to make sense of the bulging earth.

She drew the killing spade over her shoulder like a javelin. Her eyes widened as she waited, horrified, expecting at any moment a fanged head to come springing up in a cloud of dust, snapping like a dog at her bare feet. Drawing in a deep breath, she thrust the spade deep into the dirt.

She knew the snakes in that pit had been decapitated. Every last one. The freshest body in there was over a week old. She prodded the spot with a foot, feeling for any give, any softness, but the ground was solid.

Bee piled the heaviest rocks she could find over the grave, a cairn to mark the final resting place of Marie Antoinette and her army of snakes.

She rolled onto her back and stared blindly in the direction of the ceiling. Licking her lips, she wondered, again, why she hadn't just let the attorneys sell the place. Perhaps she had been so aimless that she'd simply jumped on the first path that presented itself.

"It's more than that," Bee thought, "I needed to know that I could."

She'd come all this way to prove that she could be alone, like a kid crawling under the bed to know, once and for all, that there is no boogeyman.

Bee tried to sit up. Her left arm and shoulder were stuck to the floor. She pushed against the ground with her feet, arching her back and grunting with the effort. It felt as though her shoulder blade had grown roots in the night, fleshy vines that had squirmed through the wooden planks of the house and rooted themselves in the red dirt below. Her heart drummed in her ears as she lifted her free hand, feeling her rooted shoulder, trying to find what was holding her down. Her fingers slid through a film of perspiration on her neck, around the curve of her shoulder, onto fingers.

Her exploring hand had found another, colder hand. The ball of its palm was planted firmly beneath her collar bone. Long, thin fingers cupped her shoulder. Bee's hand flew away. Panting like a sick dog, she struggled again to bring herself up from the floor. She would run to the truck, she thought. She would fly down the road, bounce through the woods, find the interstate and hold the gas pedal to the floor until she was as far from this place as she could get.

Suddenly there was pressure on her breastbone, like the knob of a knee bearing down on her chest. She kicked her legs wildly, letting loose an animal moan and swinging her free arm through the air. She searched for something to grab onto, some leverage in the dark. Through the rhythm of her heart, she could hear a humming. It was low and melodic, like a child's lullaby. She squeezed her eyes shut, shaking her head and trying to will herself back to her bed in Delaware.

The voice rattled like wind through dry leaves.

"I stepped in the water and the water was cold,
God's gonna trouble the water,"

Vowels rustled together in a breathy rasp. The words clawed their way out from whatever hellish throat floated above her in the dark. They rattled through dusty bones and hissed from ancient cavities.

"It chilled my body but not my soul,
God's gonna trouble the water,"

The mouth breathed damp air into Bee's ear. It was sweet and sour and repulsive, the smell of fermented fruit and wet rot. Cracked lips grazed her ear lobe, and her ribs gave slightly beneath the oppressive knee.

"Wade in the water,
Wade in the water,
God's gonna trouble the water."

With a shrill scream and one final thrust, she propelled herself from the floor and flew from the Den. Every nerve trembled as she lurched toward the pickup, throwing open the door and locking it behind her. Bee ran her hands over the steering column, feeling her way to the ignition. There were no keys. Her fingers crawled over seats and into cup holders. Thick sobs lurching from her stomach as she realized the truth. Her keys were in the house.

Nausea was rising, rolling like a wave and knocking against the back of her throat. She was too afraid to open the door. She vomited into the floorboard, retching and coughing until, empty and exhausted, she found sleep on the seat of the truck.

The morning sun blazed through the window, its light cooking her exposed legs and already sunburned face. The acrid smell of bile rose like steam to her nose. Bee opened the door and swung her feet to the ground. The entrance of the Den gaped at her like a hungry mouth. She couldn't bring herself to go inside, not even to retrieve the keys. She closed her hot eyes and shuffled down the hill. She didn't open them again until she was standing on the pier. Her reflection wavered below, studying her from the pond's surface with hollow eyes.

She looked away, staring into the trees and listening to the world around her. Birds. Insect noises. Dry leaves rattling against each other, hanging on to their season for as long as they could.

Tsk,tsk,tsk,tsk,tsk.

Bee's breath caught in her throat. The sound was growing, swelling toward her from the Den.

Tsk,tsk,tsk,tsk,tsk.

Her knees trembled wildly as she moved her toes to the edge of the wooden pier.

Tsk,tsk,tsk,tsk,tsk!

She told herself it was her imagination, the deafening rattle behind her head.

One roughly callused fingertip traced the line of Bee's spine down her long, bare neck. Saccharine breath warmed her ear as a dry ribbon of a tongue wormed over her lobe, playing in the fine hairs of her jaw.

Bee leaped forward, arms out to embrace whatever lurked below.

She let herself sink, trying to find the bottom. The water was cool, and she drifted away from the glow of the sky above. She sank deeper, letting bubbles escape past her lips and warble toward the surface. The song in her head played in a loop, and the words began to emerge from the tune.

"Wade in the water
Wade in the water children ..."

Sanctuary

Lauren Mason

New guy came yesterday, wet-fresh
from the scrub-down room with a side jab
to his step that put us all a-skitter.

Stab-wound Star caught him a sharp one
through the gate with her good back leg –
he was flaring and snorting straw-prongs

like she'd pissed his feed-sack,
but stopped headbutting the bars real quick.
He wasn't ready to join us, was so rough

he couldn't even stop eating long enough
to dung, just stood there chomping and messing,
carrying on like some half-breed hinny.

Hook-toe Smokey and the other boys
stood guard, a line of side-eyes, not budging
a hoof, until old Storm flicked her ears,

sent ripples of bristle and bray through the yard,
which broke like drink in the slop troughs,
one tongue at a time – Our Song.

It was clear he'd never sung before, poor guy,
sawing away like the rusty warehouse door
– heee-haaw, heee-haaw –

Sturnidae

Setareh Ebrahimi

The murmuration   looks
   like   iron filings
manipulated   by magnets.
It looks   like   punctuation.
   It swells,   then gives way
to itself,   the body   of a jellyfish.
It sucks up,   then   exhales.
   Look   how it   mocks
      our   dimensions,
   this   sky whale   paddling
   on the   horizon   where
it   becomes   smoky,
      questionable or   too real.

It's a   young   woman
in full   command   of her body,
   sitting   on her side,   languid,
   half thinking   in   words.
Each   individual   bird
   illustrates   her   curves,
alive and   constantly   moving.

This is not like   animations
where   woodland   creatures
      pull   a   princess's ribbons.
She   explodes   spectacularly,
a   firework,   to come   together
again.   She   draws   messages
in the   air,   every   shift
the swipe   of calligraphy.

The   amniotic   sac
      of the   sky   is pregnant
and we   feel   only   an echo
      of what   is to come,
          a   heat   transfer,
like   the   imprint   left
      when   a   person   presses
themselves   against   glass.

Rut

Ian Steadman

When Sasha shouts for me I'm lying slumped between the barrels, a black bag of rubbish supporting my back. If she were to walk down the stairs to the cellar, into its dim, musty world, she would probably assume I had fallen. An ambulance would be called, my pulse would be taken. The doctors would shine their skinny torches into my eyes again, telling me to follow the light, follow the light.

I have not fallen. I'm simply resting, and daydreaming.

"Cedric? We need you up here, please. Tables to clear."

My name is not Cedric. I should make that clear. They call me that, but it has never been my name. One of the customers, the barflies, called me it once, and the odour has followed me around. Thinking on it, it may have been Gary Chiltern. He's in here most nights, and every time he calls me "Cedric" he spits it out, the taste of it unpleasant on his tongue. It would be in his nature to label me with something distasteful. I add it to the list of insults he has hurled my way.

"Cedric! Today, please?"

Unfurling from the floor, I push the rubbish bag against the wall, nudge the barrels aside. I may be scrawny, but I've hauled enough beer to have some strength in my shoulders, across the lean muscles of my chest. Once, I found a stuffed stag's head down here among the bar towels and paper napkins, still attached to its wooden mount. Holding it up in front of the mirror, I imagined myself as some beast of legend, a British cousin of the minotaur. My arms and legs are stick-thin, though, and this homespun myth crumbled. I lowered the stag's head and regarded myself with familiar self-loathing: my face narrow, my cheeks hollow.

I can't afford to lose this job. So I must stack my arms with lipstick-smeared glasses, wipe the sticky, stale residue from their tables. These are the acts that allow me to eke out an existence, to keep a roof above my head.

After the cool of the cellar, the bar is bright and busy, an eruption of sights and smells. Beer and disinfectant and cheap perfume. Once I can bear to open my eyes, I see Chiltern and his gang gathered at the far end of the bar. The one they call Popeye, his biceps grossly inflated to the size of a baby's head; Flynn, the skinniest of the bunch, his neck stained blue with dense inkwork that defies unravelling. Two of the ladies are with them: Chiltern's wife Melissa and Popeye's girlfriend, Mandy Dawes. My father knew hers, many years ago. We played in the same sandpits for a year or two. I have the photos, in the box I keep under my bed.

"Oi!" Chiltern shouts, raising his hands in the air. "He finally surfaces! Where have you been, Cedric? Spitting in our beer, eh? Pissing on our peanuts?"

They laugh and I lower my face. This is the way it works around here.

Sasha is laughing with them behind the bar, her hand tight around the pumps as she pulls another round.

"Get lost down there, did you? The tables upstairs need clearing, and then there are glasses outside that need to come in. When you've done that, five needs changing too."

She tosses me a cloth and I catch it, ignoring the droplets it spits in my face. My nostrils flare at the stink of the bleach.

"Yeah mate," Chiltern says, "my dogs are tied up out there too. Take them some water, will you? Nice one, Cedric. Chop-chop."

Without a word, Sasha pushes a metal bowl along the bar towards me.

I hate Chiltern's dogs. I don't like dogs in general, but his in particular fill me with an unreasonable anxiety, a gut-churning fear. They're pit bulls, or something similar, the muscle packed tight beneath their skin, their eyes small and hard. One of them went for me once, sparking an outbreak of laughter around the bar, and they've never forgotten it. They know they own me, just like their master.

I take the bowl and half fill it at the tap. Night is starting to creep in as I push through the door, the air cold with the ghost of winter, but the daylight is stretching, grasping for the summer. There is a cut grass scent, fresh and green. At the edge of the light I can see the tall, dark mass of trees that mark the start of the woods. With shaking hands, I edge towards the two animals growling by the fence, my eyes cast down, watching the ripples in the bowl.

My dad grew up here, on the border of the common, the edge of the woods – and his father too. They walked the same paths between the tangled masses of brambles, rested their backs against the same ancient elms. Dad worked as a signalman on the railway line but he spent every spare moment outdoors, fetching wood for the fire, foraging berries and small, tart apples in the summer. I'm told that his father – my grandad – used to know the locations of all the badger setts, the best places to shoot rabbits or pigeons. I have this photo of him, faded now to shades of grey, his back against the thick trunk of an oak with a gun cocked over one arm, as casual as if it had grown out of the wood. I look at it sometimes and try to imagine how it must have been, to be at home in nature like that, to have lived in a time when the outdoors was part of your world. This place has changed since then. The world has turned. But the trees still hang on, reminding us of what once was, of the garden we have lost.

Dad used to tell me stories of the deer that roamed the woods, when he was a child. The way you'd steal glimpses of them through the trees, their tails bobbing white. His father would track them, following the trails of young bracken nibbled to the stem, picking up their scent of must and vinegar. Unlike the rabbits and the pigeons, he wouldn't kill them. They were the guardians of the woods, he said, the beating heart of the forest.

In all the time I have lived here, I have yet to see a single one.

I still live in the house that my grandfather owned, but only half of it is mine. My mum and dad sold off the first floor in the early nineties, to cover his debts. There is someone else living there now: a young man, constantly on the phone as he rushes out in his suit each morning. I can't remember his name. He floats above me, his feet never touching the ground.

At first the late-night walks were simply a way of clearing my head after the shift at the bar, winding down from the day. Then they became something more. Without knowing why, or how, I follow the paths and tracks as they weave through the trees, tracing a route that runs through me. It changes from night to night, but I can feel it tugging me this way and that, navigating via signs that I am barely aware of: an ancient elm, a clearing, a scent upon the wind. Sometimes I end up following a shallow ravine that runs through the forest floor, a dried-up remnant of some past flood, its bottom still boggy and damp. Other times I wander seemingly at random among the ferns and saplings. I imagine that these are the trails my father followed, and his father before him, that I'm walking the maps etched into my genes, but I have no proof. Maybe I'm just escaping from the twenty-first-century drudgery of my life. Maybe I'm just losing it again.

Sometimes I snatch a fistful of young bracken as I roam, the way my father taught me. These days the fiddlehead ferns are reserved for posh restaurants up in the city, but back in his day, in my grandad's day, people took sustenance where it was offered. The young shoots are almost sweet, bursting piney and green between my teeth. You have to take care, though. I remember him telling me they were poisonous in sufficient quantities, spiking your bloodstream with toxins that would make you hallucinate and, eventually, collapse. A little can keep you alive; too much will kill you.

Maybe it explains what I saw that day. It's almost four months ago now, maybe five – before the winter set in. A Sunday evening, the sunlight lancing through the trees, casting ever-changing patterns on the ground. My feet felt light, barely disturbing the scattered leaves. I remember stopping at a large oak, its bark scarred and pitted, a landscape in miniature. My gaze passed down the trunk, through the wooden valleys, to a hole that drilled between its roots. It wasn't a large hole, perhaps a foot across. Maybe a badger's sett, I thought. There were leaves and twigs scattered around its edges, a few dried brown cups left behind by last year's acorns. I could see only a few inches into the hole, then there was nothing but darkness.

It's tough to recall the exact sensations now. I remember my sight blurring, my skin hot and cold at once, as if I was about to be sick. The scent of the woods suddenly rose around me, rich and brown, the smell of compost and rotted leaves, of animal scat and decay. My head floated. The world span.

Then, without warning, there was light.

Everything was washed in sunlight, the living radiance moving between the trees in waves and ripples, swelling and ebbing. I was almost blinded, not by the brightness, but by the variety. Colours and shades roiled before my eyes, and I wondered if this was it – if I was about to die. The ghost of the bracken rose in my throat, and I tasted my father's warning.

And then I saw him. Walking through the trees thirty, forty feet from me, a colossal man, as tall as some of the trunks that swayed apart to allow his passage. As he stalked in and out of the shade he would vanish from sight, only to re-emerge into the sunlight, a glimpse of muscle here, of branching antler there. Given my condition I couldn't be certain that I wasn't imagining him – but there was the smell too, a ripe stink of animal and man, sweat mingled with a vinegary musk and a clinging, damp odour like moss. His torso was bare, a loincloth of sorts around his waist. But from his shoulders upwards the skin turned to pelt, dark and shaggy, topped by a giant stag's head, antlers branching to the sky.

He turned to face me and his mouth opened in a bellow of challenge.

In that moment, I passed out.

Chiltern and his gang are the last to leave. They let the door swing shut with a crash, cutting Gary off as he says something about taking the dogs for a walk, letting them sniff their way around the woods. There's a whoop of laughter from one of them – Flynn, I think – then the mutter of their voices fades. The night falls silent.

"Right," Sasha says, the glasses rattling as she loads them into the washer, "let's get this place closed. All the tables upstairs need wiping, I'll take the bar. I want to get out before midnight."

I don't mind closing time. Without the people cluttering it, the bar feels spacious, calm. The tables are all real wood, knotted and lined. They were probably imported from somewhere north of here – Scotland, the Russian steppes – but they bring me closer to the trees. There is nature here, even if it isn't ours.

Someone has left a woollen jumper under one of the tables. Light blue, a handful of sky. I consider keeping it, taking it for my own. I can barely afford to buy clothes these days, and the nights are still cold, the winter clinging on in the small hours of the morning. I tell myself that there is nothing wrong with foraging to survive. But I place it behind the bar, tucked into the cubby we use for lost property, as Sasha does the final checks on the till. They'll come asking for it tomorrow, I'm sure.

Sasha barely looks at me as she locks up. When she's done, she glances over her shoulder with a muttered "See you tomorrow". Then she's gone, walking quickly up the well-lit path to the Cranstone Estate, her hands pushed deep into her pockets.

I stand for a moment, filling my nostrils with the cool air. Then I walk towards the woods.

Tonight, my path is almost straight. I can feel the thread leading me somewhere, although I don't know where. The trees are growing closer here, the trunks wider, and I am aware, somehow, that I am moving nearer to the heart of the woods. Something stirs in me, raw and primeval. Without thinking, my hand snaps the tightly-curled head off a fern and I rub it between finger and thumb as I walk. Touch my fingers to my tongue for just a hint of a taste. The dry leaves whisper beneath my feet but otherwise everything is still, the air lying cold and heavy.

Then I hear voices.

They are too distant to make out what is being said, but they are undoubtedly human. My pace automatically slows, my feet treading cautiously. It must be gone midnight. I have never met anyone out here during my night walks before, and the possibility worries me. There has always been a purity to the night-time forest, a silence that's as timeless as it is rooted in the moment. Usually I can daydream that the modern world has yet to happen. But tonight, something is wrong. It's as I creep closer that I make out Gary Chiltern's voice. I know it too well for there to be any doubt. He's laughing, and the sound triggers a fear in me that prickles across my scalp. The Chilterns of this world do not belong here.

There's another voice, a woman's. I assume it's Melissa's at first, but I quickly realise that it's different, a touch higher, more nasal. I can't place it, so I shuffle forward, trying to make them out. Chiltern I can see, the heavy bulk of him pushing somebody up against the trunk of a tree. His hands move across her and she laughs too. He steps to one side, adjusting his stance, and I glimpse her face in the shadows. Not Melissa, then. It's Mandy – Mandy Dawes, Popeye's girl. The girl I used to share a sandpit with, all those many years ago. Her skirt has ridden up around her waist, and as I watch, Chiltern's rough, unsubtle hand pushes up beneath its folds. His other hand tugs at his belt and then his buttocks are bared, two pale moons in the darkness, and she laughs that laugh again, her own hands helping him. There's a grunt that can only be Chiltern's, a deep, animal sound, and Mandy gasps.

Something in me senses the danger of what I'm seeing and I start to back away, retreating into the densest part of the woods. But my heel catches a dry stick, and with a sharp *crack* it announces its presence – and mine – to the night air. Mandy's hands immediately move to smooth down her skirt. Chiltern tugs up his jeans as his head snaps in my direction. I try to remain still, my breath snagged in my throat.

"Is there someone out there, Gary? Did you hear it?"

Chiltern mutters something about peeping toms that I can't quite hear. His back is to me as he moves around the trunk, bending low to the ground, his hands busy as they loosen a knot.

"Don't worry, love," he says, his voice finding a way to me through the undergrowth. "The boys will sniff him out."

Then, black bullets, the two dogs shoot out from behind the tree and I'm running, crashing through the bracken and the brambles, their thorns tearing at my coat. I can hear barking behind me but I have no clue how close they are, whether they have found my scent. I have to assume the worst. Wherever I am, there's no way I can make it back home from here, so I let my instincts guide me. The stink of sweat rises from my body and I wonder if I have always smelled like this; if my nose has become more acute, or if the fear has made me reek. Either way, it seems infeasible that the dogs will not sniff it out.

My calves are stiffening but I hurtle on as best I can, branches whipping my face. The barking sounds close behind me now, the snaps and cracks as twin bodies career through the undergrowth. Without knowing how, I have found the shallow ravine again and I follow its course, my feet sticking in the boggy ground as I run. Perhaps on some level I hope this will hide my scent, but all I feel is the fear pumping through me, the need to flee, fast, to put some space between me and my pursuers.

And then, to hide. The thought comes to me unbidden. I can't outrun them, I can't make it home. So I must hide, and hide well. Somewhere they won't find me, or won't be able to follow. Somewhere safe.

The ravine pushes uphill for a short time, and as it does I think I hear the barks falling behind. When I reach the top of the incline the ground levels out, but in front of me lies a massive, sprawling bramble patch, at least twenty feet wide, its thorny tangle dense and unwelcoming. The dogs will not dare to follow me in there, I think. Dropping to my knees, I find a low tunnel beneath the massed branches, where a fox or maybe a badger has made its path. I push my nose to ground. My back catches on the thorns as I wriggle inside, so I drop even lower, my belly in the dirt, pulling myself forward with my hands. Something scratches the back of my neck but I carry on, inch by inch, until I must be at least seven or eight feet inside the bramble patch. I tentatively lift my head and nothing pricks it, nothing tugs at my back. Slowly, cautiously, I pull myself up into a crouch.

The dogs are circling outside. I can hear them testing the edges of the thicket, the restless padding of their paws on the leaves. There's a growl from my left, so low I feel it more than hear it. A sudden warmth in my groin and I realise that I've wet myself, the sharp stink of piss mixing with my sweat as it stabs at my nostrils. I curl my fists and squeeze closed my eyes.

There's silence for a second, two, three – as if the wind has dropped suddenly, the woods quiet and still, everything holding its breath. Then, to my surprise, I hear a whimper of fear to my left, followed by an echoed whimper straight ahead. Both dogs are simpering now, high-pitched and submissive. For the first time, the fear I sense is not my own. I hear a loud creak, like a tree uprooting itself, then a soft, wet *thud*. The animal noises stop and there is a second *thud*, even louder than the first, underlined by a sharp *crack*. Then it's quiet again.

I wait for what feels like a minute or two, although it may be longer. Time has concertinaed with the hormones fizzing through my blood. When it's clear that the dogs have gone, I drop to my belly once again, the warmth in my crotch now cold against the earth, and wriggle back through the bramble tunnel.

The first animal is waiting for me when I emerge. One of Chiltern's pit bulls, lying black and heavy on the ground. Its head is unnaturally flattened on the side facing me, and as I watch I see lines of crimson starting to seep through the fur, joining together and pooling as its blood drips onto the forest floor. Looking closer, its hind legs bend at unnatural angles, snapped in at least three places.

The second pit bull is behind it, hauled into sight as I rise to my feet. It's suspended a good ten feet off the ground, the broken branch of an oak piercing its belly and emerging through the shattered ribcage on the other side.

When I spot what I believe to be its intestines swinging from the branch I'm finally sick, the contents of my stomach forcing their way out without warning. I'm sick again and I spit, washing the acidic aftertaste from my mouth. It's then that I see him. He's barely visible between the trees: a large, dark mass in the shadows. A breeze rustles the leaves and moonlight falls upon a giant chest, muscles speckled with patches of velvet. Antlers branch into the canopy overhead, the heat of his breath shimmering about his nostrils. If I hadn't already soiled myself I would be doing so now, but instead I shiver in my wet trousers, my stomach hollow and plummeting. My thighs are already stiffening with the burn; I don't know if I can manage another chase. Without warning he bellows, a roar as loud as any bear's, guttural and wild.

Then he pushes his way back through the woods, merging into the shadowy undergrowth, leaving me standing in my piss and my vomit and the rapidly spreading pool of blood, while all around me the trees whisper to the dark.

When a magician

Kate Wise

pulls a rabbit from a hat, no small child
is amazed. For, why not?

It was late August, which had surprised us.
The earth gave up a hole
suggesting mouse at most. And yet,

between tear of bramble, burnt leaf and wall
you were rabbit;
soil-grey against greyed soil, and then soil only again.

How you scream and writhe
for freedom, shrieking *mother*,
until resigned; brief calmed to my palms,
whorls of hair yielding to clumsy thumbs

– thistle-puff down on a day of drifting seed –

and then again hips and ribs churning squeamish
against me. And I am afraid to hold you firm to flesh

nub of shoulder blade
where wings might bud
flutter-stabbing

and you boyish strong and awkward
struggle away

scutting to safety.
Abracadabra.
Then soil only again.

Palavas-les-Flots

Paul Stephenson

Contrary to widespread belief, flamingos are not pink
on account of beta carotene in their diet of brine shrimp,
but because they are massive fans of Barbara Cartland.

Be honest,
it's not for the sand at Palavas
but the view coming back late afternoon, the spectacle
from the local bus as it crosses the lagoon:

the glimpse of flamingos poncing about, wading
like nonagenarian novelists in Languedoc, tanked up
on vitamin supplements and made-up romance,

who, in chiffon and blush, mix a cocktail of schmaltz,
whisk you off to stables in storms and private tennis clubs,
where limbs fling, loins thrust, slam, volley, lunge.

Yes, it's to catch them flamboyant, mingling at sunset,
each on one leg, swaying as they plot their follow-up romp,
busily oblivious with so much pillow palaver
to life on dry land in Palavas.

Notes for the "Chronicles of the Land That Has No Shape"

Frank Roger

Prologue

In a few introductory chapters a brief overview is given of the earliest recorded history of the period prior to the foundation of the First Kingdom.

For countless generations a primitive, unorganised culture of amoebae led a peaceful and rather uneventful existence. However, self-awareness gradually increased within the community, eventually growing into a society with the faintest outlines of a structure, and the first intimations of a hierarchy.

A process of revealing and rather disconcerting discoveries and subsequent name-giving ensued: their environment was named the Pond Without Shores, their own territory was labelled The Land That Has No Shape, and the individual at the top of their fledgling hierarchy was proclaimed their first King.

Despite the worldview-shaking evolution it lived through, the First Kingdom was but a modest precursor of what was to follow, an epic story told in three volumes.

✳

Book I, Birth And Ascent: The Shapeless Brilliance Rising From The Depths

The first chapters chronicle the slow but steady ascent of the amoeba culture, as a quick succession of Kingdoms with an increasingly tight hierarchical structure relentlessly explores its immediate surroundings. For the first time in amoeba history, they encounter life forms other than their staple of food in the Pond: a variety of unicellular organisms, mainly paramecia. None of these life-forms are organised in a culture, and hence they are not considered to be a threat to the Kingdom.

Yet these encounters, however unspectacular, lead to a growing self-awareness among the amoebae, and the first hesitant steps are made towards an "amoebisation" of the Pond Without Shores, which is viewed as their own private territory that no inferior species are entitled to soil with their presence.

However, the weak Fifth Kingdom fails to live up to the general population's desires and expectations, and after a brief but turmoil-ridden period, the last of the Kings is brutally removed from the throne, and the rebels proudly proclaim the First Empire. Their bold plans for an all-out amoebisation of the Pond and a bright future for the Empire of Amorphia, as The Land That Has No Shape has now been officially called, foreshadow what is to come.

The vigorous new leadership, brimming with ambitions for expansion, exploration and the quest for knowledge, is responsible for a steady ascent of amoeba culture: its positivism, its pride-fuelled and future-oriented approach lead to a veritable quantum leap in Amorphia's history, and to a consolidation of the Emperor's power base. The old monarchy is forgotten; a bright future seems to be beckoning.

✳

Book II, Hybris And Nemesis: Holy Greatness Tumbling Down Into Darkness

A vast number of exploratory voyages are made, leading to a vast accumulation of knowledge and the blossoming of science. The Age of Enlightenment is in full swing. The world the amoebae live in appears, surprisingly and contrary to traditional beliefs, not to be limited to the Pond. Not only does it become clear that there is a lot of water beyond their own Pond, but this entire expanse of water turns out to be teeming with a stunningly wide variety of life-forms, wider than ever thought possible.

Initially, opinions are divided within the amoeba society: some believe they have stumbled onto an unlimited food supply, whereas others feel they have encountered competing civilisations on the same level as theirs, and still others are convinced they are dealing with potential enemies, and drastic measures are called for.

Certain strata of the amoeba culture are unable to cope with the dizzying pace of change in their society and the shakedown of their worldview prompted by the new discoveries, and a severe case of future shock is the inevitable result.

While the progressive forces are riding the crest of the wave of change, more and more movements arise that look back rather than forward, and that discard the countless new questions asked rather than trying to find an answer for them. Knowledge and science are rejected, and old myths and legends form the basis of various new cults with rapidly swelling ranks.

Before long, Amorphia is divided between radically opposed factions: "liberal" amoebae, intent on embracing the vast new world they have discovered, hungry for knowledge, discussing whether peaceful coexistence with other species would be a more desirable alternative than simple colonisation, and, on the other hand, "reactionary" amoebae, who support a return to traditional values, unwilling or even unable to stride into the fearsome future, and preferring to idealise a glorified past, blinded by fanaticism. At first there is a balance between these two camps, but quickly the scales tip, and the onrushing tide of anti-progress forces pushes the "liberals" into the position of a dwindling minority.

Religiously inspired cults proliferate. The Emperor does not even try to stem the tide of this menace to society; he is solely interested in his own pleasures, wallows in sheer decadence, and is too weak or uncaring to react as the reins start slipping from his pseudopods. Anarchy inevitably ensues.

A fundamentalist movement, the "Cult of the Holy Pseudopod", led by a shadowy figure known as His Shapelessness, unleashes a witch-hunt against anything or any creature with a fixed shape, considered to be a personification of evil, which must hence be rooted out. The Cult wishes to cleanse the Empire and restore traditional amoeba values, and can do so unpunished. Its success is characteristic for the spirit of the times, and many other similar movements arise.

As a plethora of revolutionary and counter-revolutionary movements forge alliances, fight out rivalries and settle disputes, more and more cracks appear in the Empire's structure. An all-out civil war shatters all dreams of greatness and makes the Empire crumble ingloriously. The last Emperor, a feeble and self-centred monarch too decadent and corrupt to even care, cannot avoid the Land That Has No Shape from sinking away into the Dark Ages.

A few strongholds of reason, well-hidden and secretly organised in order to stand a better chance at survival, serve as guardians of science and knowledge, and as a beacon of hope for the future, prepared to step back into the light as soon as the dawn of a new age of enlightenment is heralded, another chance for amoeba civilisation, a Second Empire feverishly dreamed of by a handful of believers.

Book III, Hope And Recovery: An Armada Of Shapelessness Washing Upon The Shores Of Fate

Slowly, gradually, over a period spanning many generations, amoeba civilisation rises from its slumber. The former Empire now consists of countless small principalities, that are suddenly and brutally made aware of their vulnerability as the vanguard of an army of paramecia reaches the outer territories of the motley mosaic that was once The Land That Has No Shape.

Faced with this common enemy, most principalities are convinced of the need to unite, fully realising they will be annihilated if their individual military efforts will have to make the difference. When a number of the stronger principalities, most notably those who had secretly guarded the knowledge of bygone days, decide to take command and proclaim the Second Empire, only a few die-hard religious radicals refuse to cooperate and join forces.

Their claim, once a commonly held belief, that the rim of the mythical old Empire is actually the Cell Wall of the Supreme Amoeba which no inferior species can possibly penetrate, is no longer taken seriously by anyone, and is discarded as a remnant of Dark Ages' superstition and pseudo-science. The new Emperor wishes to consolidate the Second Empire's foundation, and does so by means of a lightning-quick and efficient attack against the paramecia. These withdraw their forces, taken by surprise by this unexpectedly strong and reunited opponent, and the Emperor builds upon this success without losing time, going from strength to strength.

The entire Empire is swept along by this new elan, and unprecedented new heights are achieved in science and philosophy. New exploratory voyages are undertaken, on a vaster scale than ever before, and stunning discoveries are made. The Empire is now expanding rapidly, and many colonies of inferior creatures living in the Pond Without Shores are swallowed by it, or "embraced by the imperial pseudopods" as the official expression goes.

As imperial explorers venture far away to chart new territories, they stumble onto the biggest revelation in recorded amoeba history: the Pond Without Shores, which was always believed to be an infinite expanse of water, based on the dogma that nothing could possibly exist beyond the Pond's strictly theoretical Rim, does indeed, shockingly, appear to be finite, and beyond the Rim an even more shocking phenomenon is discovered: Dry Land, a bold new concept, a territory veiled in mystery.

The realisation dawns, chillingly, that a simple name change of the Pond Without Shores will not suffice: the amoebae's entire world view, their whole philosophical angle of approach towards life and the universe and their place inside it, generations' worth of thought and accumulated knowledge will have to be reconsidered.

All too quickly it becomes clear that these recently uncovered mysteries will not be unravelled in the immediate future, as even the most intrepid amoeba explorers find it impossible to tread the Dry Land, for it proves to be lethally inhospitable, an environment as amoeba-unfriendly as imaginable.

Still, this treasure trove of knowledge, tantalisingly out of reach as it is, fuels the pursuit of science and leads to a veritable revolution in philosophy. Indeed, the discovery of dry land has tremendous philosophical ramifications, and has brutally shattered the world view that was accepted, by all strata of amoeba society, as verified fact for the entire course of amoeba history. The resulting watershed upsurge of science, philosophy and art is truly a milestone in amoeba history, undoubtedly the biggest turning point ever reached. The Empire will never be the same again.

Book III concludes with questions such as: has amoeba culture now reached its acme? Is danger lurking in the Dry Land? How long will the Empire sustain its current position? Is a decline now inevitable, as there is no place left to go but down? And if not, what exactly is looming on the horizon of the Second Empire's existence?

Epilogue

The Epilogue serves firstly as a wrap-up of the trilogy, and secondly leaves a possibility of a sequel trilogy, should the first trio of books prove successful.

As it becomes increasingly evident that the Second Empire is not free from corruption and nepotism, the much-maligned (and prematurely presumed eradicated) Cult of the Holy Pseudopod rears its ugly head again, possibly as a counterweight to progress coming too fast for some and obliterating a lot of traditional beliefs and values still cherished by certain strata of society, however scientifically unsound.

Furthermore, there are intimations of another at least equally powerful Empire of amoebae, lurking at the far end of the Pond, and possibly awaiting its chance to strike the Second Empire a deadly blow. Will the two Empires eventually meet and violently clash? Will this meeting culminate in the biggest inter-species wars in recorded amoeba history?

The Epilogue ends with these tantalising glimpses of the future.

Rough Music

Jayne Stanton

My head is an attic stacked with stories,
the ones we learned before we grew voices.

We swallowed them whole at bedtime,
those cautionary tales Mother softened
with chalk and whiskery kisses.

They charmed us to sleep.

Now, on nights when their rough music howls
down the chimney, I stoke the fire
to burn their bridges,

keep them at bay.

I no longer look at myself in the mirror.
I can't bear the sight of my stone belly,
this sack of skin in Grandmother's clothing,

a lupine growl dying in my throat.

The Butterfly Factory

William Stephenson

In the half hour before the glue on the edges hardens
a technician with tweezers and a loupe has gentled
each segment of the chitinous thorax into position.
Feelers are sourced from silver wire. To complete
each imago, we stain mica grains to fill the wings
in a species-wide yet uniquely variegated pattern.

I'll switch one on. See the feelers bend, catching scent.
The compound eyes – lapis crystals set into miniature
geodesic domes, each ten thousand ommatidia – glitter
as they tilt to drink the light. The wings unfold and
shut, unfold and shut, a book with a restless reader.

Watch. With perfume and plastic, I simulate a flower.
Notice how the butterfly ripples and thrums against
the restraining bars as if begging to break free of the
cage that nurtures it. The exhausted insect slides its
tongue into the medicated syrup we use as nectar.

Thank you. Sign here. We shall fulfil your order.
One further suggestion. You have marbled eyes
with pupils black as the eyespots of an anyana.
The irises hint at other species: hairstreak green,
dark-framed morpho blue, the ochreous panes
of a grayling. Lend me your arm, let me eternalize
your genome. You'll feel just the strum of a wing.

Hibernation

Sandra Unerman

A longing to hibernate filled Alison every day, especially while she supervised playground breaks in a cold, damp wind; and over half term, stuck in her small, draughty flat or out walking in the rain. She missed her childhood walks over the North Yorkshire moors, but London had seemed liked a better career choice. How she hankered after hibernation in November, during lessons when all her pupils seemed cranky and quarrelsome. She reminded herself that she enjoyed teaching, that she relished the energy and enthusiasm of ten-year olds. But she couldn't make the words mean anything in the here and now. She was permanently exhausted, her life a grind of lesson plans, meetings, form-filling, marking, record-keeping. Her evenings offered little comfort. Too tired to cook properly, she dined on a succession of tinned food, barely registering each can's reheated contents, and climbed into bed each night, tired but never able to sleep. She wished harder than ever for hibernation, somewhere dark and lonely.

In early January, she went for a walk at the weekend and wandered round a junk shop. Nothing caught her interest except a bearskin, mounted on a dressmaker's dummy. Alison would never have worn fur or bought a fur rug. But this was too old to trouble her conscience and besides, it was not a decoration: it was an entity in its own right. It grinned at her out of the grime and gloom of the shop, the head intact, although the eyes were empty. The long canine teeth were yellow, the brown fur dusty. She took herself firmly out of the shop but turned round before she reached the end of the street.

The bearskin cost more than she ought to have spent. But she needed only to answer to herself for her extravagance.

'The drum goes with it,' the shopkeeper said. 'I'll throw that in for nothing.' The drum was in a cloth bag, a small tabor with a worn top. A circle of bare-branched trees was etched round the sides. As she turned the drum in her hands, the flickering shapes made Alison queasy but she did not refuse to take the thing.

As she unwrapped the package at home, the fur prickled, harsh and warm against her hands. The head lurched up and for a moment, she saw the gleam of eyes and a wet tongue. She dropped the skin and the gleam vanished, so it must have been a trick of the light. Now that she was committed to her purchase, she refused to be afraid of it. But she left it bundled in her wardrobe, until one night, when she could not sleep for cold, but was too restless to stay in bed. She padded to the wardrobe and took out the fur, trying it on in the dark.

Her face fitted inside the gape of its jaw, with the upper teeth on her forehead and the lower teeth round her chin. The grip was firm but not uncomfortable. The skin folded round her shoulders and reached down to her ankles, with the paws hanging loose. Its warmth was welcome in the chill of her room, the fur soft and strokeable. Alison sat cross-legged on the floor and picked up the drum. She was no musician but she could tap out a beat with the palms of her hands. She forgot the neighbours as she drummed and the rhythm grew wilder, the noise louder. Her ears popped and the air squeezed her from all sides.

Surprise stilled her hands and she looked up at a crowd of faces, bear faces under a moonlit sky, their eyes alive, their snouts damp and shiny. Her bedroom had turned into a clearing between black trees. Panic launched her onto her feet but she did not know where to run, even if she could have pushed her way through the bears. They rose onto their hind legs to match her. Most of them were tall enough to look down their noses at her. Their front claws caught the light, long and heavy.

'Where is the drummer?' One spoke in a language she understood, although she had never heard it before.

'That was me,' Alison managed to say. Snarls came from all sides, loud as motorcycle engines. But none of the creatures touched her and her fear eased a little. Bears who could talk might be less likely to attack, impossible though they were. She might have been dreaming, except that the stink would have woken her up, a mixture of hot bodies and fur with the fish guts and fermented fruit on the bears' breath, strong enough to clear a drain.

A different voice spoke, dark and slow. 'Not you.' This was one of the largest bears, a grizzly, she thought, nearly twice her height. 'Small he was, the drummer, but not as small as you, with a cold smile and a cold heart. He killed the daughter whose skin you wear. Did he send you here?'

'No,' she was glad to say. 'I never met him.'

'Did you steal his drum?' This bear was shoulder height to the other and had a dent in one ear.

'I found it, along with the skin.' The bear language did not seem to have the words to describe her purchase and she had no desire to explain what a junk shop was. 'The hunter wasn't there.'

'He wouldn't have let it go, not while he was alive,' said the grizzly. 'And he has not summoned us for years beyond count.'

'Then he is dead and we are free of him,' said Cutear and all the others growled in a deep thrum of satisfaction. 'Did you call us here to give us that news? What reward would you have for it?'

'I didn't mean to call you,' Alison said. 'I didn't know I could.'

'All the better,' said the grizzly. 'Drum for us while we dance and maybe you will earn a reward for your music as well as your news.'

She did not believe she could play well enough but she dared not argue. She tucked the drum under her arm and tapped out a lopsided beat as it came into her head. Some of the bears began play-boxing to the rhythm, others dropped down on all fours and tumbled over one another like cubs. They spun round one another or alone, the bulky ones as nimble as the leanest. Their eyes shone and their claws glinted as they reared up or sank down, in and out of their shadows.

Frost nipped Alison's feet but the heat from the bears filled the clearing, so that the rest of her was too warm. She could not count them but they crammed the space between the trees, bears of all sizes, pale or dark, shaggy or smooth. The fur she wore weighed down her shoulders and the loose paws flopped awkwardly, out of time with her rhythm. The faster she played, the tighter grew the bear's skull round her face. The teeth chafed her forehead and dug into her chin. Sweat stung her eyes.

A bear reared up beside her, Cutear, so close that she could see down its throat and smell its rotten teeth. 'Now we know how to reward you.'

Before she could flinch, it licked her naked cheeks and lips. The tongue of another bear rasped over her feet, another kneaded her breasts. Another and another pressed all round her, almost lifting her off her feet. They licked her in long, steady sweeps until she could no longer drum, or think or breathe. Her body changed: bones thickened and shortened, large teeth erupted painfully in her mouth, claws emerging from her fingers. She had become a bear herself. Now her head was free and the fur was part of her, itchy but weightless. Her balance shifted and her legs were stubby and strong, her nose bewildered by a surge of new, intricate smells. The drum fell from between her paws.

The bears scattered in different directions and Alison was alone. The moon had set but the stars gave enough light to show her a cleft between steep rocks, beside a spring of water. She drank deeply and pushed herself through the cleft into a small cave. There she lay down and fell asleep at once.

Hunger woke her, back in her human skin. She was on the floor of her bedroom, with the bearskin underneath her and the drum by her side. Pine needles were scattered in its fur, which looked cleaner and glossier than when Alison had seen it in the shop. She opened her bedroom curtains and stared at the leafless trees down the street. She felt as though she had slept the winter away but the dark morning looked like January still. When she checked the date, she discovered that she had worn the bearskin for only one night.

She did not mind. She was more invigorated than she could remember, even from her childhood. She dressed in a hurry and went out for breakfast. She relished the sting of rain against her face and the click of her shoes on the pavement. Black coffee, toast and pastry tasted so splendid she had to blink back tears of gratitude.

After a day's teaching, she went home still ablaze with good humour. She half expected that the bearskin would have disappeared but it lay where she had left it, with the drum on the floor beside it.

She did not need to put it on, she realised. Her desire to hibernate was sated. But the rhythm she had drummed for the bears niggled just out of reach in her mind. She wanted to play it again and to feel the touch of their tongues.

Once she was ready for bed, she put on the bearskin and sat on the floor. The grip of the jaws round her head felt rougher tonight and her hands were clumsier as they beat the drum. She fell into a muddle several times when she tried to play. At last she settled on a simple beat and kept at it, until her palms were sore and her head ached. She almost gave up, before the strong scent of bear filled her room and the grizzly's great bulk appeared in front of her. Last night, she had drummed herself into the forest. Tonight, this presence in her room was much more alarming, too large, too wild.

She could just see the gleam in the bear's eyes as it lowered its head to hers.

'You haven't the powers of the hunter, to draw magic from our dances,' it said, in the bear language. 'If we transform you again, you will become one of us and never be able to leave. Will you come?'

She wanted to say yes, to drum her life away, mate with a bear, sleep in a cave beyond the reach of anyone she had ever known. But her class would miss her. And, to her surprise, she also wanted to stay behind, to find out what she could do with the rest of her life as a human. She had had more practice at being human: she ought to be better at that than at being a bear.

Her hands dropped the drum before she knew it and she tugged the bearskin over her head. By the time she was free of it, she was alone in the room.

She stumbled into bed, too exhausted to think about what she had done. In the morning her mind was clearer. She had better not keep the bearskin, she decided, or she would be tempted to use it again. She would not sell it but find someone to give it to, someone else in need of hibernation, this winter or next.

Jellyfish

Megan Pattie

She wishes not to be a jellyfish:
a lightbulb always flicked on,
unstoppable brain
dribbling thoughts
in tangled strands.

Not to have this heavy head
she can only hold up
in the dark
underwater.

Not to flounder
on dry land:
ungainly blob,
tendrils trailing,
helpless.

Not to be
this plucked eye,
always weeping:

"Do not touch me.
Please, do not
touch me."

Barred Owl

Kristin Camitta Zimet

4 a.m., the street lamp's yellow eye
fixes the cabin: cots, ravine between,
bench like a plank bridge,
the heater's stiff blue tufts,
the floor scraped, hand-hacked,
rough as our family can go to ground,
deep as we soft ones scratch.

Feather-cowled, a barred owl's,
my head on the down pillow
could swivel all the way round
to zero, the egg that hatched me,
if I let it; I could float over
my body, pellet of fur and vertebrae,
wrapped in its blankets like an amulet.

I want to glide above all tribes of me
the night looses: scuttlers, skulkers,
all secret nosers burrowing
to earthen black from air's looser black,
all rabbity twitchers, brushtailed slinkers,
tent-skinned gliders,
clingers upon black oak.

But the laboring of human breath,
my husband's and my sons', snoring
like mallards squabbling in swampy sleep,
the gusting of pumped air,
pant of motor and scrabble of watch
are a fur of sound, rough to swallow,
over the hot silent heart.

It is muscle I want,
what moves us deep in red undress,
the blood chasing its tail
in desperate loops as talons constrict.
So I rise, stuff nightgown under coat,
hood and boot myself owl-round, and sail
out of the wooden box, the human nest.

The sky's arched primaries are brushed white;
the earth snow-breasted, streaked,
running with shadows.
Now I hear her: cousin, sister, self,
the barred owl strikes up her jackal yap,
her crusty howl.
I swoop to answer.

Ouroboros

Douglas Thompson

Derek and Amy meet in the Fox and Butterfly pub. Do you know it? I should insert descriptive phrases here, but do I really need to? Maybe we all make up our own mental pictures of pubs, instantly, before we even realise we have. That's probably one reason why they give them those traditional names. The Queen's Arms, The Queen's Legs, The Pig and Whistle, The Flying Fuck. I say a name like firing a starting pistol, and hey presto you'll see brass gantries and mirrors and optics, dark wood panelling, framed black-and-white historical portraits of local scenes. Polished floorboards, a real fire if you're lucky, but only in winter. It's not winter now. A river nearby, or maybe a canal. A wagging wave of greenery always visible at the window from within the dark interior. The vague smell of beer and floor cleaner. A distinct buzz at certain times of day, after work, early evening after the local offices come out, or when the youthful Friday and Saturday night countdown starts warming up. A distant clicking from the cues and balls on the pool table, always located in an area up or down by three unnecessary steps from the rest of the interior. The juke box will play *Nights In White Satin* at certain key moments of wistful angst every evening from now until doomsday, never reaching the end, although at any time at which you're actually enjoying yourself you may not notice this.

Amy is walking by an abandoned canal. Long grass, rusting metal, old railings and gates and *capstans* and *bascules*: such musical words, long since overgrown, passed beyond human understanding like the corroding artefacts they once denoted. She hears a soft swishing noise and looks over her shoulder. Keeps walking. Hears the noise again. Stops this time, turns around and looks all about, waiting. There's something moving in the long grass. A glimpse of an orangey-brown back moving stealthily, almost unseen, unsee-able even. A fox. It should be avoiding her, but she senses, believes, that it is keeping pace with her, coming closer even.

It's so humid. No-one is around. She strips down to her underclothes among the fireweed by the disused cast-iron sheds, her bare feet on the rough concrete, oddly hypnotized by the glimpse of her own dark silhouette, her reflection in the almost-static canal water. She lies down in the heat, in a clearing among the tall scrub, enjoying the cool dust on her skin. She closes her eyes, feels the sun on her face, begins to lose track of time.

Eventually she becomes aware of breathing, just audible above the sighing grasses swaying in the wind, the gentle lapping of the canal water against its ancient stone banks. She opens her eyes suddenly, as if someone has spoken to her, without sound or words and yet directly into her subconscious mind. She finds she is looking straight into the yellow eyes of the fox dead ahead, peeking out into her clearing from a gap in the tall knotweed. Its pink tongue is hanging out, saliva gleaming, dripping to the ground.

What animal are you? Amy asks, sitting up in bed, eloquently naked, her skin like that of a leopard or jaguar somehow, flowing, liquid, perfect. More than a covering, a suit. It's an essence, Derek thinks, her soul rolled out flat like pastry and wrapped around her, the ultimate cloak, cooked to perfection, her warmth, burning hot like an oven inside. The skin is her. He presses his nose into her stomach, the small of her back, her neck, testing this flawless envelope which both contains and expresses her. I'm a butterfly, she says, you do realise that, don't you? Gone today, here tomorrow. Shouldn't it be the other way about? He asks. No. Mind your own business. You'll understand in the end. By the time it's too late. I'm living my life backwards. You're just a leaf, a flower I'm alighting on. Wonderful word that: *alighting*. Like flitting. And flirting. We could create a new one: flittering. Yellow sunlight filtered by flickering gossamer wings. I'll always leave you, you know. Over and over again. You'll never find me, except in the past, in what has never been. What animal are you?

I'm a pig he says, at last, searching for truffles, his nose and lips running across her, as if he is pursuing her soul across the endless desert of her skin. Like Diana the huntress pursued by Zeus, turning herself into a tree. We'll change places in the end, you realise that, don't you? You'll become so depraved that you sit alone wearing old pairs of my panties. Drink your own semen just to find out what it tasted like for me.

How did it taste? He asks her. Like snotters from your nose. Like nothing special. Like someone else's spittle with a pinch of salt. Like thin chicken soup. Like big fucking deal. Sex isn't interesting, she says, going to stand at the window and part the blinds, gaze down at the dismal urban dust below. It's only what it isn't that's interesting, don't you get that yet?

No. He lights a cigarette. Looks for his watch, wonders if she's hidden it somewhere as usual, under the white sheets, the snow, the slow carnage of sleep. How do you mean?

It's a metaphor that won't work, won't fit. A drink that makes you thirsty. Like we're trying to change places as we struggle against each other, push through each other's outlines. Animals just fuck. But we, us lot, we search for gateways, portals, a thousand doors that go on slamming, one after the other. But something always drags us back breathless before the end, exhausted, down long undignified corridors, like an elastic band tied around our waist. The sinews of the heart, twisted into a cruel net by the fisher of men. From which no one can escape.

✳

Derek and Amy meet in the Pig and Butterfly pub. It has such a lovely and clever little graphic, on a sign outside and on all the menus. The pig has his snout upturned, just touching the butterfly, ever so gently, as if he's just chanced upon it in a summer meadow. And his mouth is upturned at the edges, in that very touching way that pigs have, as if they're smiling most of the time. And maybe they are, incredibly.

We really ought to be nicer to them, Derek says, tapping his finger on the picture at the head of the menu. Churchill loved them. He'd often go and sit with them for company during World War Two. He said pigs treat us as equals. He does the voice for her. Dogs looks up to us, cats look down, but pigs treat us as equals. Like maybe they know us better than ourselves.

I'm not a butterfly anymore, she tells him. He raises only a single eyebrow in response. I'm a swan. A beautiful white swan of elegant long neck and exquisitely soft feathers. I fly occasionally, she tells him. I can fly. I know I can. But mostly I just float, sail, in a slow stately way, like royalty. Royalty in old black-and-white films lost for a century in someone's abandoned attic. I choose to sail and be reflected in still water.

Fair enough, Derek says, and stubs his cigarette out. I saw a weird photograph once, he begins to tell her. It was horrible, and it was in the most unexpected place. Some prissy little rural magazine, one that posh people buy. I was on holiday with Agnes. He knows he shouldn't mention his wife or Amy will sulk and talk about David. But he knows it's all lost today, like it's all lost every day, sooner or later. *Scottish Field* or something like that. I find myself reading it in some pretty little holiday cottage waiting for Agnes to finish doing her hair so we can go out or something. And there it is suddenly. I've stumbled across this colour photograph that some reader has sent in. I stare at it for the longest time. It fascinates and horrifies me. It's of a fox and swan, both dead together under the shallow clear water of a lake, entwined around each other. And this reader wants to know, wants the editor to tell him, what the hell could have happened to these two. The dimwit. I know instantly what happened. One look at it and I know. They were fighting, the fox jumped the swan but the swan fought back. And they were perfectly matched for strength. Incredibly rare maybe but it must happen sometime, eventually, like rolling a double six. The fox's instincts told him to put his jaws around the neck and just hold on and on. And the swan's instincts told it to try to drown the fox by thrashing him over and taking them both deeper and deeper under the water. The fox is starving, it's the middle of a hard winter. He knows he needs to kill. The swan knows it needs to hold its breath longer than the fox, even if it passes out. So they both drown. It's horrible and beautiful, that final pose that they're frozen together in for all eternity. Is it an embrace or a mutual-suicide? And what's the difference in the end anyway? We've all got to go sometime.

Derek and Amy meet in the Pig and Swan. Do you know it? Only the queen's allowed to eat swan, you know, Amy laughs, one of those archaic laws like being allowed to shoot Welshmen after dark with a crossbow on Tuesdays. Shall I ask why they don't have Swan on the menu? I wish the fucking queen was on the menu, Derek mutters, we could chop her up and feed her to the swans, the blood-sucking parasite. The jewellery would make her sink. Do you know the bullets bounced off all the diamonds sewn into the dresses of the little Romanov daughters, so then the Bolsheviks had to bludgeon them to death with their rifle butts? They didn't want to be cruel, they just weren't expecting indestructible victims, like glittering white bullet-proof angels.

Swan song, he remembers, after a long unexpected silence in their conversation. What was all that about? A myth? That some species of them doesn't make a single sound all their lives until they're starting to die and then they release some melody of otherworldly beauty. Something to do with Leda and Zeus again. Those Greeks were sure into bestiality and god knows what all else. And chimeras: the inevitable monstrous outcomes of such unnatural unions. Maybe we are all chimeras. Half in half, scoundrels who've survived the womb by merging with our own dead twin.

Back at the empty flat. The sweat, the late summer night heat. The traffic quietened down like it's purged itself of its endless and aimless malice for an hour or two. Maybe we are portals, Derek says, standing up and going over to join her at the window, scarcely caring anymore what anyone might see of them through the Venetian blinds. Links to another dimension. At birth and death and this too. He touches her lightly between the legs. The laboured breathing, the flickering eyelids, the way time changes and stops. It's when we make bridges out of ourselves towards some parallel world. We think we're trying to reach each other, but all we reach is our own death, complete the circles of ourselves. *Ouroboros*, she sighs, I've always loved that weird word. How's that? The serpent eating its own tail. We try to escape our own bodies, but we can escape nothing. Except maybe time. Briefly. For a moment. An eternity. Same difference.

Derek and Amy meet in the Fox and Hound Pub. Do you know it? Of course you do. It's a much more normal and believable name for a pub than any other. It's familiar as hell. Like fish and chips, salt and pepper. Men and Women. A pattern you can't escape, which will always keep re-asserting itself. You can fight it, tell yourself it's hackneyed, too obvious, old-hat, but that won't do any good. Not for long. Not in the end. You'll never think yourself outside it. We're all just cocks and balls and cunts and tits swinging around, looking for ways to collide with each other, over and over, like waves breaking on the grey stones of some endless shore, grinding away, grinding ourselves and everything else down into sand, into dust. Some people will build sand castles, but that's only child's play, day-dreaming. The tide will always come and wash all that stuff away in the end.

What's your fantasy? Amy asks. The worst-best thing you'd like to do with me? Nothing, Derek answers. I'd like to ignore you. Because I know that would hurt the most. Hurt who exactly? Both of us. Because hurt is all we'll have in the end, and you know it. That's what it's like when you're both with other people. Pain becomes a talisman, the last memento. You know that when that goes you'll finally have nothing, not a trace, not even memories. White-out.

Fox and Hound. Named after something very ancient here. Derek finds himself running along the overgrown canalside, gasping raspingly, his feet aching, his limbs getting tired. He can hear the dog packs barking behind him, the police shouting to each other, to him maybe, as if he can still hear them, as if he's not at least half-way into another parallel universe already. The panting, that laboured breathing thing, when the time-tunnels open up. He has a stitch now, like he hasn't had since he was a kid running back to school after lunch at his gran's place. But that's another age, another universe. Can't be this lad now, with the knife clutched in his hand, still dripping with blood, her blood. The panicked kaleidoscope, the tunnel of time, is disgorging him, taking him back to where he began, making a perfect circle of his life after all. Funny that, the way it's only right at the end that you see how it all fits, know what you've always known without knowing it, know you can't escape it, know you've been here before and will have to be again. Over and over.

Amy identifies Derek's body after it's pulled from the canal. The wound on her hand is superficial, but the nice sergeant will treat it with antiseptic anyway. She tells them she's a butterfly. Derek used to enjoy tearing off her wings. He just went too far like he always would one day. Like they all do in the end. Later that day she gets the keys and goes to the empty room where he used to wait for her. Waits even longer, for hours, days, nearly a week, watching the way the light changes and listening to the strange sounds of the city outside. The city like a huge wounded animal groaning, unable to heal itself. Equally unable to die. Ever-pregnant with its own still-birth. She wants to imagine being Derek without her, Derek alone and longing for her. She wants to become him. The thirst and hunger make her weak with delirium, a kind of ecstasy. She starts to eat fragments of wallpaper. Feels her face, her body beginning to merge with the wall. Branches and leaves of trees slowly emerge from her cuffs, her collar, her shoes, colonising her in stop-frame animation.

Eventually, the next time the sun rises, she finds she has become one of the trees outside in the dense little overgrown jungle of a London garden. The pet Staffordshire Bull Terrier of Mahmoud, the Turkish chef of the restaurant on the corner; comes out and sniffs her and lifts its leg. Lets go a long slow jet of warm piss right down her side, as if to claim her. He'll be back after nightfall to rub himself against her. Desperate, unfulfilled, like all the rest of us, white eyes raised, thrown back into his head, howling at the moon. The poor bastard.

Somewhere else, out of mind, downstream, miles distant, Amy's discarded clothing – her cardigan and her white linen dress – float like swans, drifting, slowly twisting and turning. A kind of dance, stately, water waltz. The dress unfolds, reaches out as if yawning and stretching. It will become waterlogged at last and begin sinking. Unseen, beyond all human knowledge it will vanish from the light at last and begin the unfathomable descent towards the riverbed, the soft sediment of a million other unspeakable and discarded things. Mute witnesses to a civilisation that lost its will to know itself. Stopped tending the garden and let the snake back in. Slept and dreamt a deep languid dream while love became war again. I told this story, not because it mattered but precisely the opposite.

The Great Eel of Jazz

Amanda Oosthuizen

He slithers into my acoustic meatus,
and just as I'm in the groove, he glisses
through my inner ear, squeezing against my timpanic
membrane, pulsing his breath, flicking his tongue
at my cochlea, tantalising my ossicles with his blue
notes and flattened fifths.

He jangles his bebop and boogaloo
and Cuban charanga, his killer-diller
microtones of mouldy fig; cross-rhythms
mutating until my eyes squint.

I spill my fine sweet sherry onto the hole
in my jeans and the great eel of jazz
slithers from my ear and laps up the spillage,
twining round my ankles, making it impossible
to move from his greasy skin. In the low lights

all I want is the blessed memory mattress of my bed;
but the sounds of the great eel of jazz are one time,
one time only. Once snarled in his anguilliform
off-beats, nothing is ever the same again.

University Library

Lindsay Reid

Thick and black,
clustered like rooks,
books hunch on their perches.

I have studied here six long years,
heard them rustling their pages
when I turn my back.

If I sneak a look
they attack in a flickering storm,
hooking my hair.

The stacks rise to dizzying peaks.
The books have feathers, claws and beaks –
they aim for the eyes.

Vulpine

Tarquin Landseer

At heart I am a fox
that seeks a counterpart.
The mask is all him
while I wear a false face
in make-believe.
Without pretence
he is truer than me
with my self-deceit
and lapse from grace.

In this altered state
I can shift my ground,
more alive couched side by side
in the damp field
with its gift of undersound;
then watch him sidle off
through a muse
into the wood's hidlings
where he enters the earth
pure in every instant.

Out here in the withdrawn
I can dream up what's
voiced in his raggy bark;
while elsewhere
my life seems counterfeit
forged from comfy lies.

My play-acting betrays
a stand-in for what's real
as he fetches a circuit
rich in a keenness of being.
If I could take a spark
from the vital flame of him,
where in his eye-glance I see
the brighter part of what I picture,
share his stance in tact
with nature's instancy.
Then perhaps the distance
might collapse.

Sloth

Elaine Ruth White

I am hung, slung
like a cedilla,
my wide gaze
fastened
on the yard scene
below

the path, the pool,
the poor man toiling
in his glasshouse,
stained cracked fingers
poking soil around pips
and stones,

pride, greed,
each seed named
as he plants it,
lust, envy,

man moistens his lips
looks up at me,

I unfurl, uncurl
my limbs,
leave one resting place
for another
then speak to the man
in his own language.

Flock

David Hartley

Imagine it was you.

You could have been doing something profound, like walking along the canal-side contemplating divorce, or attending the funeral of your best friend's child. Or walking free from a three-year jail sentence, or celebrating the patent of your invention with a picnic for one in the park.

But perhaps you were doing something more mundane. Hanging out the washing. Bringing in the bins. Walking home from work. Let's say it was this. Let's say it was mundanity.

You were hanging out your washing, hoping the clouds would give you a stay of execution, when you noticed the swarm of birds whipping panicked shapes in the sky. These were the starlings, murmurating, and you had never seen such a magnificent display.

You moved to the end of your garden for a better look. This was your innocent mistake. That simple movement, that snag from mundanity to something briefly profound, singled you out. The starlings painted a single frame of your watching face in the air, too quick for you to see, then cascaded down and swallowed you.

Remember it? The sudden strike of a million wings on your skin, the skittering shriek of their voices deep in your ear, the wrenching of your hair as the boldest ones grabbed what they could to stop you running? You tried to run, tried to bat those things away and stunned a few, remember? There were two or three of them left behind in your garden as the others lifted you away; black blotches against your lawn like sudden molehills, the last you would ever see of the place where you lived, and ate, and slept, and cried, and loved, and smiled. Just like that.

The starlings took turns holding you, not that you noticed. To keep the momentum of the murmuration going, they had to synchronise with each other, to think as small parts of one whole unit. So, whenever a change of direction was needed, which was often, some would let go and others would dart into place to keep you held. All you knew of this were the tingling pinpricks of claws piercing flesh which, at the time, you put down to a ferocious anxiety of your nerves.

You were fortunate, though. Yours is a coastal town, so the starling journey didn't take long. They carried you over the town centre, and the nature reserve, then executed a gut-flipping plummet over the cliffs, down to the beach. Here they landed, the whole mass of them at once, and you too, face first, and the sand banked up into your mouth. The starlings let go and you spent a moment vomiting the beach back onto itself while trying to rearrange your brain back to its rightful order.

On the cliff edges, seven magpies cackled at the scene. Five flew closer, attracted by the silver on your wrist and embedded in your ears. They strutted up, planned their approach and then darted in and pecked at the metals until they came away. You didn't have the energy to fight back. I think, in the end, you helped them. Three of the five flew away with your trinkets winking in their beaks. Two remained. They wanted you to feel joyous. Did you? I think, at that moment, you were a twisted wreck on a polluted beach and it was hard for you to think much of anything at all. You just wanted to go home, correct? But where exactly is home for a human? We have never been quite sure.

The magpies took to wings and flashed away. Perhaps you thought that was it. Perhaps you thought it had all been some elaborate avian thievery to take away your shiny things. We decided it was best you don't have things to remind you of where you once were. That's all.

The gulls descended from the thermals. They were not so gentle.

The passage over the ocean was rough. The gulls, not as keen on working together, kept cawing at each other and dropping you from their beaks. You smashed into the waters more times than you can remember (it was twenty-three), and each fall felt like being hit with an igloo. It shattered you, the smack of brine, the plunge into the murk, and then the frantic ripping of clothes and skin as the gulls hoisted you back up again, sodden, dripping, an ice block just melted.

They had to learn patience that day, the gulls, which is a remarkable achievement for them. So, that's something at least, isn't it?

They took you to this place, to The Island. They circled it a few times, to allow you to see it, get the aspect of it. High mounds of guano at the edges which ringed my mountain in the centre, thick with jungle along its slopes. A hazy ring of cloud obscured the peak and an orchestra of shrieks, chatters, caws, and keens rose from every which place and all wheres.

I got my first glimpse of you. Just a distant shape drooping from tired beaks, but the sight stirred me. My peacocks helped me from my nest and I waddled to the edge of the plateau. The gulls are not worthy to approach, so it would be some time before we were brought together. But you were here now, and I could start to call you mine.

I watched as the gulls chose a place to alight. Right at the furthest point of the Western edge. It stank. You're used to it now, but remember the first time you smelt it? Remember how it pierced the top of your throat, how it reached down and gripped your lungs, how it seemed to burn the walls of your nostrils? Remember retching so hard your rib broke?

The boobies and gannets did not understand. They hobbled in as the gulls took their leave and prodded at your prostate body. They nibbled at your scalp and slapped at you with the webs of their feet. It took hundreds of them to get you to smarten up, waken up and move out. You were coddled inland and, as you reached the treeline, an albatross barrelled into your back and sent you flying into the jungle. You turned on it, remember? Ready to fight back. Ready to take on the afterlife and every demon it would fling at you.

You had no energy, though. And this isn't the afterlife. But you were so close, at that point, to death. We're sorry about that. We were as gentle as we could possibly be.

I'm sorry it was you. If it hadn't been you, it would've been someone else. Happens all the time. You had a family didn't you? Kids? A partner? Parents, yes? And best friends, lovers, colleagues? Didn't we know that? Of course we did. But you have to understand something, River; we need you more than you need us. So, we have to have this arrangement you see. It's for the best.

The parrots took you next. Gentle wings mended you. They brought food, kept you company, tried a few words of your language. Toucans brought you fresh water held in their beaks, which you managed to sip a little of each time it came. As your senses returned you contemplated a dash back across the guano to the final forgiveness of the sea, but the albatross stalked the edge of the jungle and you could not. You just could not.

Birds of Paradise coaxed you deeper into the jungle. They flitted past like living fireworks and your frazzled brain followed the colours until you were hopelessly lost among the vines. You thought you saw snakes, spiders, poisonous frogs, but there was none of this. There were only birds. Strange to think of it that way, isn't it?

The jewels of the jungle kept you salivated and they led you along a weaving path to the mountainside. Far, far above, I waited, an exemplar of patience. You lay upon the slope and begged for rest.

A kettle of vultures swept down. They placed delicate wings over your eyes and granted you the deepest sleep you ever experienced. You were weightless.

When you woke, you were with the hawks and the eagles. They flew alongside you, wings outstretched as if reaching out, as if trying to rest the tips of their feathers on your shoulder to say; *it's all going to be ok.*

Their calls echoed off the mountainside and their tick-tock eyes watched you and watched for food. For those moments you thought that you had learned to fly and you stretched out your arms to show off your feathers. But you had not learned to fly. You are a human, you do not have feathers. You were being held in the expert claws of the condor, our biggest and eldest. He is an ancient, almost immortal. He gripped your waist and your chest but did not dig in the points of his claws, so you barely felt him.

He soared past where I watched and perhaps you saw me? A dark speck on the edge of a cave, flanked by my peacocks, guarded by ostrich. Exposed to all eyes. Perhaps you saw nothing of the sort. Condor, of course, was worthy to approach, but this was not the plan, not the way of things.

He wheeled down, trailed by the eagles, and set you gently upon the steppe of snow. With a little less decorum, the eagles yanked at the rags of your clothing until you understood that you needed to be upright. You got to your feet and hugged yourself for warmth. Your lack of wings became painfully clear as the blizzard winds whipped down. Condor stayed a while to protect you from the worst of it. He left as the penguins arrived.

They huddled you in, the emperors, and you all walked together as one. Perhaps you pushed yourself up, clear of the ice, and lay upright, squashed in the down of the penguins. It's what I would have done. They chattered and cawed at you, our wise old emperors, to help you understand. They told you about me and the death of my mate. About our one remaining egg, about the failures of all the others. I needed companionship, River, I needed friendship. I needed something that the other birds just couldn't quite provide.

I needed that human touch, that intelligence of care. I needed stories and poems, pictures and song. And I needed your violence, River. The crook of your finger, your steady eye, the lust of your blood.

The penguin march was slow and long, they were not so used to waddling in such a close mass. They stopped as night fell and pressed in closer, but their squabbles and skirmishes kept you from falling asleep. A few more hours of trekking after dawn and then you arrived. The emperors pushed and squeezed you out to meet my ostrich at the foot of the final ascent. Reluctant but loyal, the ostrich ushered you onto her back and carried you up to my plateau.

And now here you are.

You are a marvel. The smoothness of your skin, the finery of your golden hair. All the birds of The Island will want to see you and peck beaks at your strange little toes, the funny whorls of your ears, your extra bits of flesh. The peacocks stripped you down to see if you are a male one or female one, but we were not sure. It does not matter. I named you River.

I am not the most impressive bird. Not the largest, or the most colourful, or the strongest. I cannot fly and I do not have much hope for my last egg. Nor am I smart to the changes of our world. Do you feel it? It is hot when it should be cold, cold when it should be hot. You see why I cannot hope? Perhaps hope is something you can help with, perhaps I am doing it wrong.

I am the last of my kind unless this egg proves otherwise. This is why I have taken you. I'm sorry it had to be you, but we will take good care of you, I promise. The Island is bountiful with insects and small mammals, you will not go hungry. And loosened feathers will cover blue skin. Wounds will heal. Memories will fade.

And you will not grow bored. Here, on the eastern edge of the plateau we have mounted the rifle. A trophy we salvaged from an ancient hunting party. Finches clear away the rust and snow. The hummingbirds keep the barrel clean and crows supply bullets for the stockpile. I trust you know how it works?

Lie here. Your finger on the trigger, that's it. The stock in your shoulder and your eye to the scope. Take a moment to scan the scenery. The jungle, the guano, the plains, the coastline, yes? You will lie here watching and if the dodo hunters come, the parrots will squawk and the hawks will hover above each target.

We will allow you to rest for a few hours each night. You will join me in my nest and we will huddle together over the egg. We can grieve together and hope together. I know I will love you and I think you will love me too. Life is better here, yes? Life makes more sense here.

Imagine if this wasn't you. Imagine if this was someone else. You would be so envious, wouldn't you? To have been one of the unlucky ones, left behind.

But it isn't. It's you. You are mine and I am yours, we are a flock of two. And together, we will hope for the best.

Fishy Business

Diana Cant

In these days of water,
I drift with distaste through
long cellular shafts of weed,
laden with salmon spawn
and the extrusions of cold-eyed char.

I do not belong here;
I shrink from the bulge and slide,
the press of the hard muscular flesh
these oocytes will become,
glaucous and gelatinous.

Fertility at such a price:
give me pearls for glassy eyes
and I shall sport my gritty glamour
downstream, near the dockside,
where the flesh is warm,
where frenzy wears a human face,
where reproduction is less urgent,
and is not the only game in town.

Wojtek

Mary Livingstone

I

You came from mountains: orphaned,
sacked, passed from hand to hand,
sold to soldiers at Kangavar.
You were taken by the temple of Anahita:
Qasr-al-Lasus, robber castle. Some said
it was covered in silver worth thousands
of talents, before it was plundered,
the house of water's guardian spirit.

II

There were waters you did not know:
rising, waves wrapping the world
in their wake. You were raised on bottles
by strange men – wine, tea, milk mixed
with vodka. You ate their cigarettes like
fiery sweets. Their voices were harsh,
their legs pasty, chickenish in desert shorts.
This was rough love, wrestling on dusty ground.

III

They were prisoners too: released from gulags
to fight as Russia turned. You travelled
together – Henryk, Dymitr – to Iraq, Syria,
Palestine, Egypt. They taught you to salute,
to sleep in a tent, praised you when you caught
a spy, fed you beer and honey. Drafted you
into the 2nd Corps, painted your image on their
uniforms, gave you a name: *Wojtek, 'joyful warrior'*.

IV

You fought, chest to chest, dark and matted,
at Monte Cassino. Comrades fell beside you,
their blood-smell in your throat. Trained to copy,
you strained against the heave of crates, you
with no fear of guns. Stood, breath bated, as the road
to Rome opened – the Polish flag flown in the ruins
of abbey walls, white over red. After, they counted
the dead as you foraged for bees in the hills: thousands.

V

You were transported, your unit scattered, Poland
split. Henryk to Ontario, Dymitr to Croydon, Wojtek
to Edinburgh. Demobilised, the days turned
to years as you slowed, arthritic, a spectacle
for tourists. Sometimes you heard a Polish word,
and it drew you from your cage. *Niedźwiedź*. Bear.
Then you lost them again. Waited to be shot, alone
and in pain. They said it was a soldier's death.

*Wojtek (1942-1963) was a Syrian brown bear who was found as a cub in
the mountains in Iran and sold to the new Polish army, which was formed
of prisoners released from camps in the Soviet Union after the breaking
of the Nazi-Soviet pact. Wojtek was adopted by the soldiers and enlisted
in the Polish II Corps, 22nd Transport (Artillery Supply) Company, was
engaged in the Battle of Monte Cassino in Italy, and ultimately ended his
life at Edinburgh Zoo.*

Susheela

Bindia Persaud

The trouble started with the new headman. His predecessor had been flexible and tolerant, and the villagers hoped that he might be too, but he hadn't occupied the office for more than a week before it became apparent that he was like a bull elephant in his first musth – he had to roar and stamp just for the sake of it. Women who harboured memories of him as a fat, placid baby dandled on his mother's knee learned to lower their gaze and hurry past him, veils pressed against their faces. Men old enough to be his father's father had to petition him humbly, hands folded, as if he, not they, were the grandsire.

Susheela was the only one who didn't submit. She was a small, unassuming woman with nothing of the virago about her. Nevertheless, she had the habit of looking people full in their faces with a keen, unwavering gaze. That gaze betokened friendliness and curiosity more often than not, but sometimes her large, limpid eyes flashed contempt. Her husband Balwant knew that look from experience, knew that it left a man feeling small and meagre, so he could sense what danger Susheela was in when she turned it on the headman.

He had ordered her to fetch water. Susheela, who had been shelling betel nuts in the courtyard with a bevy of other women, got up to comply. With no great urgency, she made her way to the well. Her languor angered the headman more than outright defiance would have, and he sprung from the charpoy he had been lounging on. "Faster, woman!"

Susheela didn't reply. She let the pail drop and stared the headman down. The onlookers trembled for her, but a faint thrill ran through the crowd when he lowered his eyes first.

The punishment wasn't as bad as it might have been. The offender and her husband were barred from using the village well for three days. The headman's voice quavered as he pronounced the sentence, like that of a youth newly arrived to manhood. Even so, Balwant and Susheela knew better than to press him further. They departed for home, faces downcast.

Once back in their hut, Balwant didn't bother raising his voice in reproach. He just said, in his quiet way, "You'll have to use the far watering hole." Susheela said nothing, but her anger was evident in the vehemence with which she shrugged off Balwant's hand. The path to the watering hole was set in a declivity so steep one needed a mountain goat's sure tread to navigate it. Seven years ago, the daughter-in-law of the previous headman had lost her footing and fallen. It was the sight of her broken body that had prompted the headman to have the well built. Balwant knew that Susheela wouldn't meet the same fate. The headman's daughter-in-law had been a plains girl, and the petted darling of a wealthy family besides, but Susheela was a hill woman, with a hill woman's hardiness. The three days would pass, and so would her ire.

On the first day, Susheela awoke before first light. She set out before Balwant left his bed and was back before the sun had reached its apex, water pot full to the brim. Her hair was disheveled and she was worn out with exertion, but she attended to her other duties. By evening, nothing was left undone. That night, Balwant took her feet in his lap and massaged them with hard strokes. Before Susheela drifted off to sleep, he almost offered to go to the watering hole in her place, but he thought better of it. He was needed in the fields and fetching water was a woman's task.

At the close of the second day, Susheela asked, "Why can't I use the other watering hole?"

Balwant kept his voice very steady. "You know why."

As a young bride, Susheela had asked his late mother the same question. "It's cursed, child," she had replied.

"Cursed how?"

"It changes you. That's all I know."

Susheela wouldn't let the matter rest. She peppered her mother-in-law with questions until the old lady lost her temper. She took her

116

daughter-in-law by the shoulders and shook her slightly. "I don't know how the curse works, and I don't care to know. Stop asking. And know this – if you take even one sip of that water, you had better find another household, for this one will be barred to you."

Susheela recoiled as if she had been slapped. She wasn't accustomed to harsh words, for her mother-in-law had liked her from the start. This was a relief to Balwant, for he had been told before his marriage that four breasts couldn't reside comfortably under the same roof. He had also been told that he should never interfere in women's quarrels, so he offered no words of counsel or admonishment. His mother and his wife spent three days circling each other warily, like cats upon their first meeting, before settling into their usual amity.

Balwant knew that the Susheela who stood before him now could not be quelled as easily as that timid bride. She ran his household and had borne his sons. He couldn't simply threaten to put her out of the house, or even bid her to be silent. She turned away from him without arguing, but he knew from the set of her shoulders that she had decided to go her own way.

The next day the heat was fierce. Susheela had arisen while it was still cool, but when she arrived back home, she was bent almost double beneath the water pot, for the sun beat upon her exposed flesh like a goad. She set the pot down, spilling a little, and scooped out a handful of water to splash her face. When she caught her breath, she turned to Balwant. "I drank from the near watering hole. This water is from the far one, but I couldn't wait that long. I was thirsty and it was so hot."

Her words fell upon Balwant like a sword. He stood for a moment, trembling; then he shrugged. "What's done can't be undone," he said.

For the rest of the day he watched her, alert to even the slightest change. There was none, as far as he could tell; his wife was as close-lipped and placid as ever. After the evening meal, she sprawled on the cot with her sons in her lap. Balwant wanted to pry them from her arms, but he couldn't bring himself to do it. Curse or not, it was wrong to take children from their mother.

The air pressed in close, hot as a tandoor. No one stirred, except to slap away the flies that hummed around their heads and alighted upon their skin. Once the boys had been dispatched to their own beds,

Balwant settled in next to Susheela, "We can sleep apart if you like," she offered, but he refused. He was still her husband and she, his wife.

As she lay facing him, he heard a buzzing and spied a flash of white in the velvety darkness. Just before his eyes closed, Balwant thought that if the curse did nothing more than give his wife a propensity to snap at flies with her teeth, he could live with it.

He awoke to the sensation of being rocked. When he came to, he was no longer lying on the thin, scratchy cot, but appeared to be sprawled across what felt like an ambulatory rug. His hands clutched at what lay beneath him. This was no rug. A rug does not give off heat, nor is it underlaid with dense knots of muscle. He was straddling a tiger, his fingers buried in her brindled fur. She had stopped moving, but every involuntary twitch of ear or flank told Balwant of her power.

Balwant was tempted to hurl himself backwards, but he did not. Instead, cautiously, he started to run his hands down the length of her back. She appeared to like it, for she stretched out her paws and laid her great head upon them. Her breath was expelled in short, forcible huffs. It took Balwant a moment to realize that this was indicative of pleasure, the wild beast's counterpart to a domestic cat's purr. His own breathing slowed and his heart stopped galloping. He laid his cheek against the tiger's neck and felt himself drop into slumber.

A dream. It was a dream, of course. Susheela was wedged against him. For once, she had not roused herself before her husband. As Balwant's eyes became accustomed to the pallid light of the new day, he noticed a dark shape in the far corner. As he approached, he saw that it was a young antelope, slender legs akimbo, its neck cleanly broken. He turned and looked at Susheela. When she smiled, there was blood on her teeth.

They dressed and roasted the carcass hurriedly. Outside of feast days meat was a rarity, for the villagers needed the headman's permission to hunt and he often withheld it. Susheela dutifully served her husband and sons first, but Balwant made sure to keep some choice morsels back for her. He observed her as she settled on her haunches for her own meal. There was something lascivious about the way she smacked her glistening lips and licked her fingers. He knew then that even if she still continued to shelter under his roof, she was lost to him.

If Susheela knew it too, she gave no sign. She went to the village well for water and gossiped with the women there. She assigned chores to her sons and shouted at them when they didn't do them. She behaved, for all the world, as if she were still his wife. But how could a tiger be a wife?

Wife by day, tiger by night. As long as the sun was up, she was his own Susheela, but once it had descended beyond the horizon, she went forth to roam. Sometimes she brought back a kill, sometimes she didn't. Balwant never asked her about her wanderings, nor did she offer to tell. What he did do was look at her in a way that was new. Even when they were first married, she had never been the object of his sustained interest. He had accepted her as the pivot of his life, but he hadn't been curious about her until now. He had never noticed that her eyebrows didn't quite match, or that the fine hair at the nape of her neck grew in a whorl. He found himself greedy for these details. Not only that. Her inner person commanded his attention as much as the outer. He wondered what prompted the smile she wore at unexpected times. He wondered if she ever wept when no one was looking. And he wondered what made her the fit receptacle for a tiger. Or perhaps the tiger had always been there?

Balwant recalled their wedding night. They were both fifteen, and strangers. New brides were expected to put up a token show of reluctance, but Susheela had fought him like a thing possessed. She provoked him so with her nails and teeth that he retreated to the far end of the bed. He turned away from her and sulked until, laughing, she approached him and ran her index finger from the nape of his neck to the base of his spine. In the morning Balwant's back sported an array of thin red welts.

After the children were born, lovemaking became a less frenzied affair. At night the boys lay not three feet from them, and they had to snatch pleasure where they could. Susheela loved her sons, but sometimes her manner with them frightened Balwant a little. When they were younger they would clamber over her, small hands everywhere at once. Susheela would tolerate it, but only up to a point. When she had had enough, she would turn and pounce on them. "I'm going to eat you up," she would cry, as she insinuated her fingers into their most vulnerable spots. The boys squirmed and shrieked in response, caught

119

up in a vortex of commingled delight and fear. Once she went too far. Balwant was on his way to the fields when he heard his older son cry out. This was not the low grizzle that speaks of ordinary childhood hurts, but a ragged keening that pierced Balwant to the quick. Once he had made it back to the hut, he found his wife bent over the boy. She was running her fingernails across his ribs, and the very delicacy of the action somehow made it worse. Balwant, with uncharacteristic urgency, sprang across the room and seized Susheela's wrist. He had always thought she wasn't herself in that instance, but now he thought the opposite – a curtain had been drawn back, and he had seen who his wife really was.

Balwant was only given a month to ponder these matters. He was sure that Susheela's nocturnal peregrinations had escaped any notice but his own, so when the headman called a meeting, he thought nothing of it. He expected to be informed of an upcoming wedding or apprised of changes in the allotment of grain. Instead the headman spoke of a tiger that had been sighted dangerously close to the village's outlying dwellings. The beast would have to be driven off or killed. The headman talked further, of who would head the hunting party and the supplies they would need, but Balwant heard not a word. When he glanced at Susheela, she looked impassive, even bored.

It was almost dusk before they were in their own house again. As they got ready for bed, Balwant pondered what he should do. He could bind his wife with ropes, but could ropes hold a tiger? Could their hut, with its flimsy walls and a roof that admitted the rain, serve as her prison? Perhaps he should command her to go, but he hadn't the heart. Susheela, for her part, was quieter than usual. This wasn't the sharp, pointed silence that she sometimes employed to punish him, but something gentler, more inward. She pulled her sons towards her and bestowed more kisses than Balwant could count, on their foreheads, their hair, their hands. He was kissed too, once they were lying face-to-face, and embraced so tightly that he felt as if their separate limbs might fuse into one.

Sleep came before he was ready for it, and with it, fervid dreams. He tossed and turned on the cot until he was awakened by a hot gust of breath. A resplendent tiger was sitting beside him, so close that not a hand's breadth could have passed between them. Balwant was curiously unafraid; this was Susheela, and she meant him no harm. She blinked her amber eyes three times and nuzzled him. When Balwant made no motion to withdraw, she ran her coarse tongue over his face like a rasp. Then she left Balwant's side and went to her sleeping sons. She sniffed at them, but made no attempt to stir them. Next, she padded to the open doorway, but once there, she turned herself about, as if she could not make up her mind to go. Balwant thought to coax her into staying, but before he could cry out, she slipped away and was gone.

Balwant couldn't believe this was her final leave-taking. That morning, he buried himself in work so deeply that he didn't hear the messenger summoning him to the village courtyard. The man had to repeat himself three times before Balwant heeded him.

Once Balwant had pushed past the throng, he saw the reason for the messenger's hushed urgency. The headman, or what was left of him, lay in the middle of the square. His throat had been slashed and his belly opened. It was then that Balwant understood. A tiger that had tasted human flesh could not continue to reside among men.

At the hastily convened cremation, the only sound that could be heard above the ululations of the professional mourners was the weeping of Balwant and his sons. Some of the villagers viewed them askance; Balwant had no more reason to mourn the headman than anyone else. To a select few, Balwant had put about the story that Susheela had left him and returned to her parents in a fit of pique, and those so informed were content to attribute his tears to her abandonment. In any case, no one questioned why Susheela's disappearance coincided with the headman's death, and there was no more talk of hunting down the tiger.

The next day, Balwant took his boys by the hand and led them to the watering hole. He was almost tempted to stoop down and take a drink, but he thought better of it. What guarantee was there that he would turn into a tiger? He might transform into an antelope instead. There could be some satisfaction even in that; he imagined himself bounding away on fleet hooves while Susheela bore down on him. Then again, he might take the form of some small, scuttling thing, too insignificant for fellowship, beneath her notice even as prey. It was best to remain as he was.

He decided to stop up the watering hole instead. He moved th larger boulders himself, while directing his sons to lift and carry the smalle rocks. It was the work of a day, but they succeeded in what they set out t do. It was some consolation to know that no other man would lose his wif as he had.

Balwant never remarried. He grew more taciturn and gray with eac passing year, so that he took on the air of a grandfather long before he wa one. His sons thrived and took wives in their turn. The bright chatter c his daughters-in-law gave comfort to Balwant in his declining years, but h never ceased to mourn Susheela. When he was an old man and knew h didn't have much time left, he went in search of her. His sons followed hi tracks into the forest as far as they dared, but they soon turned back, in fea of the tiger that dwelled there.

Fluke

Michael G. Casey

Kidneys clean pallid blood
while womb of encased oyster
sighs and pulses with the moon.
A change, when gills suck in seawater
and a particle, unfiltered,
sticks fast in mucus meant to salve.
One grain of sand between shell
and mantle is all it takes to pierce
the heart of our creation goddess.
What can't be spewed must be absorbed;
nacre is secreted layer by layer until
the barb is rounded to conform, a pearl
is made, a planet like a living earth,
formed in the same way by pure chance.

Buck and Doe

Jane Burn

Little fleecy feet – velvet lucky paws dotty-dabble
moontide grass, hippey-skip, belly fuzzy-plump
from all the nibbling. Cowslip, comfrey. Busy teeth,
gnawy-gnash on root an' stump, tasty tubers relished down
in tiny gullet swallows, sweet with sugar juice.

My baby coney-kins, my leveret kith – tufty bullets
quatting in the grass, long and blowy, perfect for this game
of hidey-seek. Coloured mud like groundling truffles,
otter brown, gravel grey, knobby flash of banderole behind,
linty white. Digging thigh-bones muscled strong, footing

on the earth with knock-knocks – thumpy-stamp for danger.
Mealy unders richly warmed with down, woolsome-snug and kittened
in the stomach of our nest, our darkling womb, our holey safe place
tatted cosy-soft with dandie grasses. Elder-rabbits sage us
with fine words. *Beware the silver necklaces of snares an' keep*

away from Pink Eye with his winking froth of mixie tears.
Buck an' doe, dancing under wedding skies, kissing
clefty mouths together – mothers innards full of litter dreams,
an' hope for all her sweetly nipples hung with babbies,
sucking rich an' growing hoppish strong, foxing clever.

They make their music – open up the mallow flesh
inside their throats, slither music round their teeth.
Un-soundable to human ear but heard by cloud
and earth – this creature-sing, the joy in field and sky.
the taste of welter-song turf-spun rich upon our tongues.

A Structure of Perfect Angles

Jane Lovell

I should fly this space,
my wings flints of light stitched
in veins of winter leaf,

but how to leave her, my Queen,
unguarded and alone?

She follows me, my clutter of limbs,
around the room, her eyes
accepting of my transformation.

Sheathed in chitin, each cuttled segment
gleams like shone mahogany.
Antennae flicker as I crawl.

I scale the wall to cover, with my abdomen,
her thin frame, her beauty,
my legs a structure of perfect angles,

by the creep of shadows measure my days,
by the sounds of coming and going,
of voices I barely remember.

I grow brittle, translucent.
My limbs trap light, radiate amber.
Succinum citrinum.

Oh the elegance of death!
I am one with her, my Venus,
in this room of dreams.

Two Lost Souls

Tracey Emerson

Goldfish never blink. No eyelids. They sleep with their eyes wide open, and their teeth grow in their throats. I knew nothing of these wonders until Shelley came into my life.

We met one cold Friday night at the Give Inn, a soulless establishment just off the M1 at Chadwell Services. I arrived at reception a beaten man, armed with two six-packs of beer, three cheese and onion pasties from the garage next to the hotel and an overnight bag stuffed with packets of paracetamol.

'Hello, Val,' I said to the receptionist. She greeted me with a nicotine-stained smile.

'Hello, Colin.' Her weathered face, mottled with fake tan, made her appear at least sixty, but I suspected she was younger than that.

'Busy tonight?' I asked.

'Could be better.' She handed me the usual form to fill in and passed over the key to my usual room. 'How's the traffic out there?'

'Grim.'

'It's chilly for March, don't you think?'

'Very.' I willed her to stop talking. I was desperate to reach the sanctuary of my bland, depressing room. Desperate to consume all I'd brought with me.

'Fancy some company?' she said.

I stared at her, unsure how to reply. She'd never made any gesture of friendship before. Did she suspect my plans? Maybe others before me had killed themselves at the Give Inn and Val could spot the warning signs.

'Must get lonely sometimes?' she added. 'In that room, all by yourself.'

I noticed the pink blusher smeared across her thread-veined cheeks. The red lipstick on her chapped lips. Did she usually wear so much make-up? Sweat erupted on the back of my neck. What if she was flirting?

Val pointed behind me. 'She's there if you want her.'

I looked round. In the far corner of reception, on top of a wooden hostess trolley, sat an aquarium. I moved closer and stooped to peer inside. Fronds of fake seaweed swayed in the water. An ornamental pirate's chest and a plastic clamshell lurked at the bottom of the tank. No sign of any fish.

'Ten pounds and she's yours for the night,' said Val.

A golden tail emerged from the clamshell and flicked at me. A challenge? An invitation?

'I read about a bloke who owns a hotel in Scarborough,' she added. 'He hires out goldfish to his guests to stop them feeling lonely.'

'I'm not lonely,' I said, but my bag full of pills contradicted me. I pushed my face closer to the tank and lowered my voice to a whisper. 'I won't feel alone much longer. Soon I won't feel anything.'

Another flick of the tail. Why not have some company, I thought? Someone to witness my pitiful exit. 'What's her name?' I asked.

'I haven't given her one. No need to go that far, she's only a fish.'

The glittering tail flicked once more before retreating into the shell. I experienced a sudden and intense urge to christen the fish. To claim her as my own. I wheeled the trolley over to the reception desk.

'Shelley,' I said to Val as I handed her a tenner. 'Her name's Shelley.'

Our first night together, the night I'd intended as my last on earth, I slumped on the edge of the bed, gazing into the aquarium. I opened a can of beer and drank it whilst waiting for my companion to show herself. I felt foolish but thought, what the hell, what harm could it do? Having Shelley there might keep me focused on the task ahead and prevent me from calling Carol.

Most Friday nights, despite my best intentions, I found myself on the phone to my ex-wife, sobbing my way through a drunken declaration of love. Sometimes Carol responded with patience and understanding, on other occasions she hung up on me. I knew if I spoke to her that night, she would uncover my morbid plan and talk me out of it. I'd already written her a note, insisting she shouldn't blame herself.

'Cheers, Shelley,' I said, lifting a second can of beer to my lips.

A flash of gold. She darted from her hiding place and swam towards me. Right up to the glass, fins wiggling, her black eyes full of mischief. I felt certain she was looking straight at me. Self-conscious, I patted my stomach.

'I know. Shouldn't be drinking beer with a belly like this.'

Her fins quivered. The motion made her look like she was laughing. I almost smiled but stopped myself just in time.

'It's not funny.' I unzipped my overnight bag and tipped the contents onto the bed. The tablets I'd collected over a two-month period from numerous chemists in Edinburgh and Brighton.

Shelley watched from the water, her black eyes fixed upon my horde.

'I never thought I'd end up like this.' I explained to her that I used to be slim, that I once had hair, that at university I'd played lead guitar in a band. I gulped back the rest of my beer. 'I'm forty-two years old and look where I've ended up. Alone on a Friday night in this dump.' I sighed. 'The world's better off without me.'

Shelley circled the tank, fast and frantic. Came to a standstill at the front of the glass, water rippling around her. Why, her black eyes asked me? Why?

'My life's a joke,' I said, and out it all poured. How Premier Alliance Insurance had transferred me from Brighton to their headquarters in Edinburgh, with the result that I now spent my weekdays in Scotland and my Friday nights at the Give Inn to split up the long journey home. Home being a bedsit in Brighton, all I could afford after the divorce.

'Carol got the house. Moved her toy boy in quick sharp.' I glanced away from the aquarium. 'Suppose she can't hang around if she wants that baby.' I spared Shelley the details of my infertility – its cause and the humiliating tests I'd endured to discover it. 'Thing is,' I said, still unable to meet Shelley's eyes, 'Carol swears that's not what finished us. She says we broke up because I got depressed about it and stopped communicating with her. When she told me about her affair, I said I wouldn't stand in her way. She accused me of giving up on our marriage, but what could I do? She didn't love me anymore.'

When I turned back to the aquarium, I gasped. Shelley was floating upside down, no sign of movement. Was she dead?

'Shelley?' I tapped the glass. 'Shelley?'

She flipped back onto her stomach, fins shivering with mirth. I let out a burst of shocked laughter. She was teasing me. The fish was teasing me.

Her cheeky prank slayed my self-pity. 'Boring you to death, am I?' I said.

Shelley glided back to the glass, nothing but kindness in her eyes.

I smiled. I felt lighter, brighter, a sunrise starting deep in my belly. I looked at the heap of tablets on the bed and laughed. How pathetic. How absurd. What was I thinking?

'Sorry. No more moaning. I promise.'

Shelley's fins quivered again, and we stared at each other until my eyelids fluttered their surrender.

For the next two months, I spent every Friday night with Shelley. As soon as we were alone in my room, I would tell her about my week – funny incidents at work, annoying colleagues. Baz from Marketing did this, or Debbie from Human Resources did that. I shared snippets of my childhood too – the name of my first dog, the name of my first girlfriend, the name of my father who had remained but a name to me all my life.

When we were apart, I couldn't stop thinking about her. I searched every online thesaurus I could find for new words to describe her. Shelley, you are gilded, aurous, aureate. After exhausting all synonyms for golden, I turned to other languages. I told her she was gouden, dourado, zlatna. On one occasion, I tried addressing her by Latin name only, but Carrasius auratus auratus proved tricky to say after a few beers.

I sometimes wondered what she did all week but couldn't dwell on the question for too long. The thought of someone else enjoying Shelley's piscine affections proved unbearable, so I pushed the idea away.

Each Friday, when I drove my red Mondeo into the hotel car park, anticipation overwhelmed me. Heart pounding, I would rush to reception, where Shelley would greet me by swimming giddy spirals.

'She's always pleased to see me,' I said to Val one week, as I handed her the ten- pound payment.

Val chuckled. 'Don't be daft. Goldfish only have a three-second memory.'

My hours of research had taught me a lot about goldfish. They have a memory span of around three months. They can recognise human faces and distinguish one person from another. I shared this information with Val, who rewarded me with a sceptical look.

That night, I impressed Shelley with my knowledge of her kind. 'You originated in China over a thousand years ago,' I told her. 'You're a descendant of the Prussian Carp.' She weaved between strands of seaweed as she listened. 'I also know you can live for up to thirty years.' I stroked the glass. 'I was so happy when I discovered that.'

I feared my sentimentality might send her fleeing back to the clamshell, but instead she met me at the glass and held my gaze. A terrifying joy swept over me. Unsure what to do with it, I blinked and looked away.

✳

The following Friday, the inevitable happened. I arrived at the Give Inn later than usual, due to roadworks on the motorway. The sun, which would soon set, still had some warmth to it. The day's unseasonal heat had left stains on the armpits of my shirt, and I felt flustered and weary. I wanted only to check in and pick up Shelley but managed to delay myself further by letting my car keys slip from my sweaty hand whilst hoisting my bag from the boot of the car. They landed on the grate of a nearby drain. Cursing, I dropped to my knees and rescued them.

Disaster averted, I hurried into reception, gourmet fish food in my jacket pocket and the Polish word for golden sitting on my tongue. No sign of Shelley's tank.

'She's out,' Val said from behind the reception desk. 'The bloke in room fourteen snapped her up. She's very popular these days.'

My heart sagged. 'But she's mine.'

Val shrugged and muttered something about an online booking system to avoid future disappointment, but my thoughts were with Shelley. Did she recognise the man from room fourteen when he arrived? Did she wiggle her fins for him too?

Jealousy propelled me into the lift and up to the first floor. I reached room fourteen, knuckles raised and ready to rap, but the voice behind the door stopped me. A low, monotonous voice. This man, this stranger was talking to my Shelley, and she was listening, soaking up his sorrows.

Clutching my bag, I slid to the ground with my back against the door, tears gritty in my eyes. The man's voice droned on. I remembered sitting numb on the sofa whilst Carol confessed her affair. I remembered her sobbing and begging me to fight for her. For us.

I knew what I had to do. Leaving the hotel, I returned to my car and tossed my bag onto the back seat. Then I walked across the car park to the garage, where I withdrew three hundred pounds from the cashpoint machine. With the money bulging in my jacket pocket, I returned to the hotel and hammered on the door of room fourteen.

It opened to reveal a bald, paunchy man in a burgundy dressing gown.

'I'm from the aquarium repair company,' I said and barged into the room. Shelley bolted to the front of the tank when she saw me, tail and fins trembling. How could I ever have doubted the connection between us?

The bald man was furious. He pointed out he'd paid ten pounds for the fish and wanted his money's worth.

'It's an emergency,' I said, silencing him with two twenty-pound notes from the bundle in my pocket. I patted the side of the aquarium. 'We're getting out of here, Shelley.'

Val looked confused when I emerged from the lift, pushing the trolley in front of me.

'We're leaving,' I declared. When Val protested, I slapped the remaining two hundred and sixty pounds onto the reception desk. 'That should more than cover it.'

Val must have agreed because she snatched up the money and waved us on our way.

I wheeled Shelley out to the Mondeo and lifted the lid of the boot.

'I'll soon have you home,' I said, 'where you belong.'

I crouched down and pressed my face to the glass. Shelley hovered before me, the black discs of her eyes shining with happiness. We looked at one another for a long time.

Neither of us blinked.

'It's just you and me now.' Straightening up, I reached out to lift the tank into the car, and, as I did so, Shelley leapt out of the depths into the air, her golden body streaking past me in a high arc that carried her up and over my shoulder.

'Shelley.'

Drops of water flew from her scales as she landed on the concrete, close to the rusty grate of the drain.

'No.'

Diving to the ground, I tried to cup her in my palms, but she wriggled away towards danger.

'Please.'

With a final flip, she manoeuvred herself between the bars of the grate and vanished into the sewer beneath.

'Shelley.'

I yanked at the grate with both hands, willing it to come loose. I'd read online about the ability of goldfish to jump from their tanks, but I never expected Shelley to do it. Not to me.

'Don't go,' I yelled into the drain, much to the amusement of the man getting into the VW Golf in the adjacent parking space. He drove off, shaking his head.

I stayed there for some time, beneath the orange dregs of sunset, tugging at the grate with raw and rust-streaked hands, my sobbing lost in the ceaseless roar of the motorway traffic.

Company to Keep

at the Harvard Museum of Natural History

Jenny Grassl

Lay me down in a cotton bed like the passenger pigeon
subtracted in a box of glass, in a museum of brick,

in a city of appetite, on a planet of ghosts. Give me a number
on a tag, a few brief notes: say I was not the last human.

May the ornaments on my double helix glitter in a drawer –
moon hair and bone, one look of lust, a chain of alphabets.

Build a room around me where hummingbirds crisp on the wall,
in attitudes of flying, near my newest shoes and crabs flexing

in jars; a place for me to wake and sit astride a tortoise shell
and aim for sky, beetles pinned to my chest like jewels on a shield.

Capture evergreens. Pose immense tigers to threaten my foes
in the afterlife. Invite good spirits with trophy butterflies

and bottles holding their genitalia. Let the kronosaurus
and his teeth sink into the liberties of pretend ocean.

Make an island of my notebook, tread watery names
of the dead. Close no eyes, keep them open with forever's want.

Last night a deer

Kerry Darbishire

jumped through my window. I curled
to a warm nuzzle, fawn-scent, soft sheets
of meadowy breath slipping my shoulders

the way I sink to my neck in moss, the way I glide
bracken fellsides, graze the wild and delicate,
the way I lick trees and sky from forest streams.

But how will I make tea, drive into town, keep
to leafless concrete, shallow one-way streets?
Will people notice me shopping for nuts

and woody things, green and rooty things, picking
up carrots and cabbages in my teeth, pushing
the trolley with my nose without sneezing, without

drawing attention to my hooves tapping
the narrow vinyl aisles of tins, packets, plastic?
How will I pay, avoid the stares, those exchanges?

And through morning blankets of mist,
who will hear my bark?
How will I find my way home?

Miss Muffet Owns Her Inner Spider

Hannah Linden

I was never one for parties
after the crush at the beginning.

My siblings didn't want to stick around
any more than I did. We'd have

tied each other up in knots. I try to keep my eyes
open for them, the usual waterworks, leg it

if I see them – I'd suck the life out of them.
I'm just being honest! There's a beauty

in laying it out as it is – letting the pattern
make itself from you, naturally

then sit in the middle and wait.

Dewclaw

Ian Kappos

1.

In the summer the boy asks his mother for a dress. It is very hot out and besides he has always wanted to wear one. So his mother buys it for him. It is purple, the boy's favorite color, and oversize, so that he must gather it in bunches around himself.

He plays outside in his new dress, spinning around and around on the sidewalk, making big purple circles. The neighbor girl tells him she likes his dress, would he like to play? The boy plays with the neighbor girl until her mother offers him a popsicle that – instead of onto a stick – is frozen onto a potato peeler.

At home, the boy's mother forbids him to play with the neighbor girl. Nor is he allowed to go anywhere near the neighbor girl's mother.

One day the boy's grandparents come to pick him up. When they see his purple dress, they are upset. Words are exchanged between the adults. The boy's grandparents take him to their house, very big and in another city, and make him scrambled eggs with ketchup and melted cheese. It is American cheese. He is three years old.

When the boy is frustrated, he says things such as "I hate you" and "I'm going to kill you." This dismays his grandparents. They do not know where he learned such phrases.

※

2.

The bus is nearly full. The boy holds onto the pole, his mother next to him swaying to and fro, as if underwater. He cannot see her face.

Down the inside of his mother's leg slip two rivulets of blood. The man sitting in front of them has a sour expression. Everyone else who the boy can see is looking in another direction.

The boy looks down, lifts the tumble of his own dress, inspects his legs. No blood. He looks up at his mother, nudges her with the back of his hand. Mom? he says. Mom?

He still cannot see her face.

3.

The boy does karate. Although he is smaller than the other boys and keeps changing his nickname, he loves karate. He is very enthusiastic.

One day the other boys play a trick on him. They are all changing in the changing room, a small room behind the dojo with just enough space to change and for a large tank which the boy is told is a water heater. Here the boy must get out of his purple dress and into his karate clothes. It is not easy for him: the dress – once too big – has become snug on his body, and he has to squirm out of it.

While he does this, the other boys turn out the lights and leave. They jimmy-rig the door shut behind them. Then it is just the boy alone in the dark with the hissing water heater.

The boy panics. He is afraid of the dark. He fumbles his clothes on but does not know which is front and which is back. Then, over the sounds of his breathing and moving, comes the sound of a high-pitched cackle from the ventilation shaft above his head.

With his pants still around his ankles, the boy yanks the door open, runs across the dojo floor, and into his sensei's office. Gremlins! he screams.

In his distress, the boy trips and falls. He chips his tooth on the metal leg of a chair. He has the tooth crowned.

From now on, when he thinks of that high-pitched cackle, he will think of teeth.

4.

On Christmas Eve, the boy lies in bed. V sits beside the bed, telling the boy stories about the boy's father. V and the boy's father used to be in a band.

On the cassette deck, a tape of their band plays.

It is the best thing the boy has ever heard, the boy tells V. The boy asks if his father ever sang in the band.

V smiles wanly, says no. This disappoints the boy, but only momentarily. He can still hear it in the music, he insists. His father's voice. This puts him to sleep. The boy dreams of his father, sitting in the room with him, smiling, holding a guitar. His father looks like him but older and fatter.

Next to the tape deck, V leaves out a plate of cookies for Santa Claus. When the boy wakes up, the cookies are covered in a trembling black blanket of ants.

5.

When his grandparents come to pick him up, the boy hides his dress in his backpack. Though it is almost too small now to wear, in his nervousness he still likes to stroke the fabric.

During the car ride, the boy becomes sick. He coughs and coughs – a horrendous cough. His grandparents take him to the hospital. How long the boy is at the hospital, he does not know; everything is fuzzy around the edges, everyone's voice too bright, even when they speak in whispers about what could be wrong with him. He is given pills and unsalted meals.

When he is finally returned home, the boy goes into the bathroom and looks in the mirror. Until now a skinny little thing, he is twice his normal size. Bulges of fat have sprung up all over his body. He will no longer, he fears, be able to fit into his purple dress at all.

The boy screams out to his mother, finding then that his throat is constricted in a strange way. He is alarmed at the sound that comes out. It is a high-pitched cackle.

6.

The boy struggles with sleep. He has always struggled with sleep, his mother has told him. He tossed and turned even when he was in the crib. At night, he lies perfectly still in bed, on his back, his arms crossed over his chest, like how he saw a vampire sleep in a movie once. He does not fall asleep. He wonders if the vampire ever slept, or if he, or it, faked it.

The walls of the boy's room are purple. In the dark, once his eyes adjust, they are another color that he does not know the name of.

7.

The boy's mother's birthday approaches. He racks his brain for what to do for her. He does not know how old she will be. He has heard, from others, that she is young.

The boy procures a box. On the outside of the box, with markers, he draws different body parts, knowing that his mother likes body parts. He labels one side "vagina," another "penis," another "butt," and so on.

Upstairs lives a couple whose names he always mixes up; both are named after kinds of birds. They feed the boy sometimes, when his mother is away. The boy, proud of his work, lugs the box upstairs to show to the birds. The birds look at each other, then back to the boy. They smile faintly. He likes them.

When the boy takes the box back downstairs, he finds a pair of scissors and punctures the box. He is trying to get to the blood. He has always had an imagination. His teachers have told this to his mother. You're so creative, his mother has told him.

The boy waits, box in lap, for his mother to return home. He waits a while.

8.

The boy wants a cat. The boy's mother, in a good mood, gets one from a neighbor down the street who has many. One day the boy comes home from school and finds that the cat has given birth to a litter of kittens, all knotted up on a towel on the floor and covered in clear and red goo, mewing. He covers them with a strip of his dress that he left at home for fear of the cat forgetting what he smells like. The kittens are blind.

Don't worry, his mother tells him, they're only blind for the first few days. Then they can see.

The boy is overwhelmed with joy. He names the kittens, then, one by one, over time, he changes their names, never quite able to settle on the name that will fit perfectly each kitten's personality. One by one, as they grow older, and see, and walk, the cats disappear. One keeps coming back, though. Right now his name is Leo, and he is a tabby.

The boy enters the kitchen one afternoon to look for something to eat. Strewn across the floor are gray feathers. Leo stands next to the kitchen door, a dead pigeon before him. Leo regards the boy coolly, then walks back outside.

The boy looks at the dead pigeon. It is the first dead thing he has ever seen. He thinks of renaming Leo.

9.

On the wall of the hallway is a streak of red-brown, where the boy's mother discarded a piece of dirty clothing and it scraped across the paneling. The boy is afraid to go into the hallway at night because he is haunted by the image on the cover of David Bowie's *Diamond Dogs*. In the hallway live three blue women. They will eat the boy.

10.

Some days, when she is well, the boy's mother takes him to a place called The Needle Exchange. He does not know what The Needle Exchange is, exactly. All he knows is that they go there to help people, people who need needles. Sometimes his mother laughs and smiles and hugs and says nice things to people, handing them clear plastic bags full of little plastic sticks with little orange tips on them. Other times, his mother is only there for a short while, and brings one of these bags home.

On the days when his mother laughs and smiles and hugs and says nice things, she brings home friends. Some of these friends are women who like other women, or men who like other men, or women who are men, or men who are women. These people also help at The Needle Exchange. The boy likes when they come over; he feels more comfortable around them than he feels around most people. They are kind to him, they like his dress (which he pulls in tatters from his backpack to show them), and they think he is just such a good kid.

On the days when his mother does not leave her room, the boy looks out the kitchen window at the little shack in the backyard of their apartment building. That is where the cats like to go and hide.

What do they call it? he wonders. Their claws are very sharp, he knows. They must have no use for needles.

11.

In bed, wide-awake, the boy rolls over. He rolls over onto something wet and coarse. He opens his eyes and checks underneath him. It is vomit.

Was I sick? he wonders. But he is almost certain that he was not sick.

12.

Playing tag with his neighborhood friends, the boy falls to the ground and busts open his chin on the concrete. He watches a puddle of blood stretch out beneath his face. He cries out so the whole neighborhood can hear.

His mother rushes him to the hospital. The doctors stick needles into his face to numb the pain, but this seems to defeat the purpose; they hurt, too. It all hurts. Afterwards they bandage his whole jaw.

You were so brave, his mother tells him, wiping tears from his face. She takes him to his favorite restaurant for pancakes. He gets a triple-stack and drowns it in maple syrup. The maple syrup gets all over his bandages. His mother giggles. He giggles. Their server smiles at them.

Do you want more? his mother asks.

The boy nods yes, smiles a big sticky grin.

Later on, his mother will remove the bandages to find the stitches beneath petrified in sweet amber.

13.

Occasionally there are people over at night, and there is noise, and the boy's mother plays records. The boy's favorite song is Iggy Pop's "Dog Food." When it comes on, he dances, twirling fistfuls of grubby purple fabric, and his mother laughs, and if there are guests, they laugh, too. The only part he knows is the part when Iggy Pop says, I'M LIVING ON DOG FOOD. The boy sings along to it. He wants to try dog food, but all there is in the apartment is cat food. So he tries cat food. He likes it; it is salty. He understands the cats better now, he thinks.

14.

The boy's mother has a broom, a twisted, gnarled broom, made out of part of a tree. A witch's broom, is what she calls it. She drags it across the white-and-black checkered floor.

The boy is informed that there is a cockroach behind the stove.

The boy's mother yanks the stove forward, and out from behind the stove crawls a giant cockroach, bigger than the boy could have ever imagined. It is as big as his mother's thigh, or bigger. It hisses. The hiss sounds like a water heater. When it hisses, its wings flare to the sides, revealing beneath them wondrous patterns on its skin. The patterns look as if they were stamped into the cockroach, or etched there, by an artist.

With the broom, the boy's mother beats down at the cockroach, which is so big that it seems to struggle under its own weight. The bristles of the broom stamp new patterns into the cockroach, until its skin mingles with the pattern on the floor and creates an all-new pattern.

※

15.

The boy's mother's room is almost always locked; sometimes he does not know if she is in there or not. This time the door is not locked, so he opens it, and she is inside with B, her new boyfriend, who has replaced V, her old boyfriend.

Sitting on the edge of the bed is B, and kneeling beside the bed is his mother, with B's penis in her mouth. B's penis is big and very scary.

Is B hurting his mother? the boy wonders. B has hurt her before; this is why the boy liked V more, V never hurt his mother. But right now his mother does not look like she is in pain; she does not look like she is in anything. Neither she nor B notices the boy. He leaves the room.

He goes to the backyard. The weeds are almost as tall as he is. He clutches the top-half of his dress, still mostly whole, which with a marker he has covered in patterns so as to disguise himself as a cockroach, in case he comes across any.

The boy treads carefully through the weeds.

The ground is warm beneath his toes.

Magic, the boy thinks. He likes magic.

At the door of the shack, he listens for cats, listens for guitars.

At the eruption of noise, he holds his breath. He closes his eyes. He waits – as the high-pitched cackle, coming from the darkness of the apartment behind him, starts to get louder – for something to drown it out. And eventually, something does.

✳

16.

The boy plays with his action figures. He packs red clay into their grooves.

Yesterday, while the boy was at school, B left, taking with him the boy's Nintendo and bicycle.

The boy hopes that V will come by with a burrito for him, as he still sometimes does, but tonight he does not. The boy has not talked to his grandparents in some time; his mother told him that they are bad people. The cats come and go.

The boy needs to go to the bathroom, but the light in the hallway will not turn on, and he is scared to go down it. So, he holds it in. For a while, it even feels good. But after a time, he cannot hold it in anymore, and he relieves himself in the litter box. He wipes himself with a piece of dirty clothing and then throws it onto a hill of other dirty clothing.

Some of the clothes are not his. In fact, many of the things in the boy's room are not his.

One of his things is a bookshelf. It has his name soldered into it in big letters. The boy knows it is his name because it is one of the few words he is able to read. He is ten years old.

In addition to the boy's name, there is blood on the bookshelf. Dried spurts of it. The boy never noticed the blood before, does not know how long it has been there.

17.

When his uncle gets there, the boy has not seen his mother in days. This time the boy knows she is in her room because he has been waiting in the hallway for her.

Finally, his mother stumbles out of her room and into the glow. Her eyes travel the ceiling, the walls, fall finally on the boy.

She is so skinny, he thinks. Has she been crying? Her cheeks are wet, but she seems too dried up to have any tears inside her. But tears do come, when she embraces him. She says she loves him so much.

The boy is asked to pack all his things. His uncle will carry them down to his truck.

In his uncle's truck, leaving the city, he feels his uncle's eyes on him. Watching him stroke the mess of filthy, discolored cloth. The boy wrenches his hands from his backpack, forces himself to zip it up.

Your mother is sick, his uncle tells him.

The boy's uncle has whiskers and many freckles. The boy wonders if, underneath his clothes, the freckles form a wondrous pattern. Thinking on this, the boy cries until, exhausted, he falls asleep.

The sound of the engine turns into the sound of a purr. In his dream, the boy rides a giant cat through a thicket of weeds.

Later, after they arrive at the house, his uncle pulls all of the boy's things out of the back of the giant cat. The house is bigger than his mother's apartment but not as big as his grandparents' house. It is very hot out.

When the boy's uncle takes a hose to the bookshelf, the boy watches the water and blood pool together in the cracks of the driveway, descend to the street, into the lawn. It goes into the grass.

It will keep the grass alive, the boy thinks. That is what blood is supposed to do.

What did you say? the boy's uncle asks.

The boy looks up. He squints. In the sunlight, it's like his uncle's whiskers are not even there anymore.

Female Skate

Sarah Westcott

Who could resist
after months at sea, parched
for the rub of earth on his fingers,
the itch of spring, a river in spate –

He drew her from the wastes,
wings hanging,
her tail a bell-rope,
held her in bare hands,

felt her wetness
slipper his cassock, chest, skin,
spark a fierce blue flare.
He unhooked her at the gullet,

a nick in her throat,
lay her on the deck,
a quiet earthing,
her body shining

like cold cream.
He wiped grains from her lips,
soft as his daughters' feet, mourned
her designs, gliding lovely

towards him in those dreams,
he knelt and kissed the quiet small face,
the modest features, he prayed for her.
With rocks in his soul, he fell to work.

Note
*Some fishermen were said to have become aroused when seeing the underside of
female skate due to the apparent similarity between their reproductive organs
and human female genitalia.*

Noctuary

Tarquin Landseer

unhooked
  the flutterers are about
  stitching the owl-light
    with a sleight of hand-wings
they switch into black air
  quick as a blink

all twittery
in furtive flight
  inklings dip
to skiff the dewpond
  sip the mist

mousey microphones
turn up the silence
  tap the wires
    trace the beetle's click and tread
    then sense my being
which fills a space
  list the size of flesh
in its guise
  the stuff of hyle
before it takes shape

pips pitch above high F
  bright pinpoints
of sound that map
the dark's unseen
with half-sight
  a nose-leaf decodes
a blood heat
  feels the pulse-wave
of everything that breathes
  the haemic rush
in arteries

as they act on strays
  eldritch fur-things
cling to the night
at the chink of day
  nip purblind through
the crack between realms
  cross the mind

Her Audience Shall Stand in Ovation

Jason Gould

An Observation on the Girl in Room Ten. The last forty-eight hours have seen a marked alteration in conduct. Note deliberate use of the word *alteration*. It is too early to say if the state of self-control indicates improvement, given our lack of insight into the motivation behind the apparent shift from the disturbed behaviour observed since her admission six days ago, and her sudden tranquillity. Benefits to her wellbeing aside, it is of concern to every doctor at Longfield, myself included, that the decline in emotional turmoil should manifest from nowhere, prompted by neither medication nor counselling. Episodes of extended obsessive-compulsive behaviour seldom cease without reason. Of course, it is likely that we simply haven't picked up on it yet – the trigger behind her improved disposition. She is, however, inclined to sit quietly now, and turn the pages in one of the picture books from the communal play area. No longer does she demand pen and paper, night and day. No longer does she scribble and sob her way through endless letters of apology and guilt, addressed to her mother, wherever her mother might be. The letters have been the heartbreak of the ward. The first, read aloud to an unsuspecting staff nurse, described her condition as "an insult inflicted upon my poor, undeserving mother, by whom I was selflessly brought into the world." Other diseases, it said, might be tolerated – chicken pox, measles, mumps. But what kind of girl allowed herself to be born with an unfinished heart? In another letter, the girl said the imperfection of her heart, the hole they'd discovered, was like "the hole in a useless bucket", which had placed upon the shoulders of the mother a burden she had carried since the girl was six (we estimate she is now twelve). In the correspondence the girl attributed blame entirely to herself. She blamed herself for the money wasted on ineffective treatment. She blamed herself for the nights when sleep failed her mother. And for the further, more expensive treatment. And the antidepressants, the For Sale sign in the garden, the other woman in the arms of her father. She was in absolute agreement with her mother. It was all her fault. It was her heart, her hole. But at the end of each letter the girl made a promise. She would get better, she said. Her heart would be normal. If only her mother would come and collect her.

Me but Not Me. "You ask me that every day," says the girl. I explain it's my job to enquire after her health. Her room attracts the sun before noon but she prefers it cool and shaded, the blinds half-closed, everything striped in degrees of dark. She is sitting up in bed, the picture book to which she has become attached open on her lap. It is how I find her each morning. Today, however, I notice a hand-held vanity mirror, face-up on the pillow beside her. She says, "One day you'll walk in my room and I won't be here." Where would she be, I ask. Her eyes glaze at the thought. She says, "Oh, I'll be here. Only it won't be me." Who would I find in the bed, I ask. "Me," she says. "But I'll be different." And she lifts the picture book and turns it in my direction, and I see the hand-drawn illustration of a smiling, friendly-faced earthworm.

The Lure of Imminent Revelation. Letter-writing has been substituted by obsessive mirror-gazing. Each morning the girl holds the small looking glass in front of her face, where it remains, on and off, for much of the day. We have ruled out body dysmorphia. Initially it was our opinion that emotional trauma might account for an overwhelming repulsion toward her own physiognomy. But in studies of self-loathing the reflective surface will often be covered or turned to the wall. And

155

this is not the case. Nor has any attempt been made to deface, scratch or depower the glass. It is amicable, the look shared between the girl in room ten and the girl reflected. For several days we have watched the girl watch herself. She examines the book. She examines herself in the glass. She returns to the book. And so forth. It is our conclusion that she is drawn not by something that resides already within the mirror, but by something yet to be seen.

Fun Facts About the Worm. (1) It lives in your garden, under the earth. Unlike us, it can breathe underground. (2) A worm cannot see, but can sense light. Too much light, however, is bad for the worm. (3) Unlike us, a worm has more than one heart – it has five! (4) The worm has no backbone. If you were a worm you'd be able to touch the tip of your nose to the small of your back. (5) If the worm finds itself – My pager beeps. To the girl's disappointment I need to be elsewhere. She wants to read further. In an effort to elicit the motive behind her fascination for the humble earthworm, I had steered our daily conversation toward the picture book, and asked which of the animals she liked best – from Armadillo to Zebra. As if to justify her response she had begun to read aloud from the page entitled *W for Worm*. It is an unusual choice. It is the bird or wolf with which the troubled mind commonly associates. Fantasies of escape into flight or freedom carry an obvious symbolism. But the worm embodies qualities quite the opposite. It is illogical, the object of her yearning. Why does she long to assume such form?

In the Middle of an Anonymous Night. Nobody saw the vehicle that left the girl at the entrance to Longfield Hospital for Sick and Infirm Children. Nobody saw the driver, who did not hang around. An orderly noticed her sitting in the rain in the carpark. He put her in a wheelchair and pushed her to the nearest cubicle. They provided a blanket, hot cocoa. A nurse asked if she was in pain. The girl said nothing. She trembled under the strip-light. She pressed her back into the wheelchair as if to put distance between her and the strange place to which she'd been sent. In her face we saw the realisation that the abandonment with which she'd been threatened had finally been made real. We could all see that she'd been deliberately misplaced. None of us were surprised when we found the envelope in her coat: the medical history, the payment in cash for a period of private healthcare. But the hastily scrawled note did take us by surprise. It was not an apology or explanation but an attempt at some kind of handover, as if whoever had written it – the mother, we can only surmise – believed it sufficient to absolve herself of responsibility, not on a temporary basis until the girl was healed, but forever. Other items about the girl's person: a small valise, some clothes, a bar of soap wrapped in a towel. That first night she said only one word – sorry. Later, we realised it was meant for the absent mother.

That I Might Be the Thing I Yearn to Be. Conversion from girl to earthworm should be relatively simple. She will close her eyes, cross her fingers. And if she believes hard enough, it will happen. Years earlier, around the time of her original diagnosis, she had been told that the best cure for illness was belief. If she believed in a healthy heart, it would one day be real. She appears to cling to the advice even now. The idea that faith might influence the composition of tissue has found itself applied to an altogether less conventional goal. Her mother had believed in her. And her father. They had told her. And she tells me, now, late one night. I am working the nightshift. Like most nights the girl is awake, working on her transformation. Glancing at the picture book, open on her bed, I notice that it adopts an unscientific, cartoon-like approach to evolution. On the dustjacket a fish pirouettes on fins, a Dodo wears a dunce's cap, and a monkey in a pinstripe suit and bowler hat steps forth from a magician's cabinet, his backbone miraculously vertical. Even in the near-darkness she seems to sense my scepticism. "You think I'm childish, trying to turn myself into a worm. You think I should grow up." She should sleep, I say. In her condition she needs rest. "Help me," she begs. We are helping her, I say. We are doing all we can. "Not my heart. I've given up on that." How else might we help?

"Believe in me," she says. "Close your eyes. Cross your fingers. Help me be like the picture in the book."

An Unexpected Conscript. It seems innocent, at first, the outline of a nurse standing by the girl's bed. But as I pause at the slightly open door, I realise the nurse has her eyes closed, her fingers crossed. Light from the corridor defines the room at its most basic: bed, heart monitor, the nurse and the girl in their respective positions. That a medical professional should indulge in the make-believe world of a patient is quite irregular. The occupant of room ten will not be cured by an act of desperate superstition. Opening her eyes the nurse will not behold a half-animal, half-human hybrid. The girl's arms will not fuse to her ribcage. Her legs will not become ring-like segments. Her eyes will not seal over. Breath will continue to pass in and out of her body through lungs, not skin. Her backbone will not dismantle. And she will walk on two feet, on the human side of the earth, happy in sunlight, not push herself through dark soil on microscopic bristles. The birth-form cannot be switched. An organism does not hold inside itself the cellular pattern of an alternative organism that might be summoned at will. Perhaps the staff at Longfield need to be reminded of the fact. It is of concern that the action on behalf of the nurse – to join the girl in her unhealthy pursuit – might grant credence to the conceit, if only in the mind of the child.

Sudden, Inexplicable Hope. The aberration on the girl's left wrist proves unusual in both texture and colour. Underlying blood vessels do not appear to be ruptured. A translucency, the size and shape of the disc on a stethoscope, enhances the visibility of the vein-junction beneath. Pigmentation in the affected zone appears to have altered. The result is an opacity or, at least, the illusion of opacity, as if the skin has become thinner. Cause has not been identified (Longfield does not employ a dermatologist), but psychosomatic tendencies remain the probable diagnosis. Expecting the obvious reply – that the skin-mutation signifies the start of the metamorphosis – I ask the girl what she thinks the mark on her wrist might be. Light fills her eyes, and she says, "A sign my mother is coming."

Disciples of the Worm-Girl. Rumours abound regarding events in room ten. People gather in the silent, subdued atmosphere of the room they've heard about, motivated to the girl's bedside by their willingness to help in a cause they consider benevolent. To all intents and purposes they believe their participation altruistic. How can they not be part of it, they say. She was abandoned by her mother, with her heart in tatters – literally. Poor thing, they say. Poor, poor thing. All she wants is to start afresh. But why a worm? You'd think she'd want to be something more graceful. Despite the ignominy of her desired future-state, they close their eyes and cross their fingers. And by the bedside they channel their belief. A low hum is said to be audible if a large number has gathered. The lights in the corridor flicker – or so the story goes. And a mild, not unpleasant tension – akin, perhaps, to the excitement that foreshadows some grand discovery in childhood – twists itself into the abdominal muscles of everyone present. And they all hold their breath, the way infants hold their breath in the moment before the big surprise bursts from the box. But in the morning (the meetings are nocturnal) the girl is still the girl. It might be all talk, but if it is more than that – if these happenings actually occur – then it represents a breach in security. Staff on the wing in question have been interviewed. It would seem the minor society that has sprung up owes its subscription to Longfield employees, though in recent nights the circle has widened to include friends and relatives and even the public. A construction worker in high-vis tabard, for example, is said to have told the nightshift nurse, "If it was my kid in there, I'd hope people would help." An elderly gentleman turns back at the door to room ten, unable to enter. He himself, according to the witness, aches with the need to transmute – to wake in the body of a bird, to hop from his mattress and fly away. A female ambulance driver – intrigued but sceptical – is reported to have said, "I thought I was wasting my time, but I swear she arched her back to an impossible angle." The tales go on. If it is not curbed, it will grow, this following. It suggests that if we try hard enough we might be different. An attractive prospect for many. Action must be taken. The nurse thought to be the original conscript will be suspended with immediate effect. The ward will be locked overnight. Room ten will be checked every fifteen minutes for intruders. And a memorandum will be issued reminding staff that it constitutes a disciplinary offence to collude in the girl's ambition to be an invertebrate.

"Listen to My Foot." As I test the girl's heart, a twice-daily procedure due to her complaint, I hear her speak, muffled and distant. The reading complete, I update her notes and remove the stethoscope. When I ask if she spoke, she says, "Ventricular septal defect." Correct, I say. I ask how she learned this term. She shrugs. "You haven't finished," she says, as I bend the stethoscope into my pocket and turn for the door. "The first of my new hearts came to life last night. It's in my left foot." She nods at the book of animals on the bedside table. "It's a little known fact that a worm has five hearts." She beams radiantly. Her foot appears from under the bedsheet. "Listen, if you don't believe me …"

Love is an Inconvenient Concept. "Longing to transform from human to animal is longing to be excused from humanity, to exist outside its protocols and practices." Theories on the girl are under scrutiny at her case review. "In other words," my colleague continues, "if the girl was a worm she would not care if her mother was cruel or decent, evil or good. The animal kingdom does not attribute qualities the way we do." Another colleague suggests it might be a coping mechanism. "The girl knows she might die and be buried. To become the creature by which she will be advanced upon might offer some degree of comfort. In her mind, she'll be the bigger worm, the eater and not the eaten." Someone asks my opinion. "Philosophically speaking," I say, "the girl can be anything she wants to be." Somebody says I sound like a convert. Have I been standing in her room at night, he asks, with my eyes closed and my fingers crossed? Ignoring the remark, I say I stand in partial agreement with the first prognosis. The animal the girl covets is related to the mother. But we do not understand how, or why. In some way, the transformation is meant to make the mother happy. And can there be any nobler cause, any greater gift, than to unseat sadness from another human being – your mother, or anyone.

The Wayward Tendencies of Mother Nature. A delicate heart – the latest of the five to defy anatomy – beats behind her right knee. In too much direct sunlight the skin on her left forearm peels away, and raw muscle is exposed. It affects her respiration and the team fit her with an emergency oxygen mask. Sometimes her body curls back on itself, in skeletal collapse, shoulder-blades to calves, ears to heels, the soles of her feet curved about the nape of her neck. She roams the moonlit grounds of the hospital. She perfects the technique of abdominal transportation. In the morning, after a night in the soil, her bedsheets give off that rainwater-reek, clumps of earth stick to her scalp, and on the lawn the caretaker bags up girl-sized worm casts. One day we find her in the artificial vivarium of her shaded room, devouring the root of a withered pot plant. From afar, if glimpsed through the frosted glass of her door, for example, she appears ruddy and slim, a slinky, human-sized S, slow in motion yet laden with an ancient significance.

Still No Word from the Authorities. Although the circumstances surrounding the girl were reported to the appropriate agencies when she first arrived, an officer was not despatched with the urgency anticipated. Furthermore, the attitude displayed by the officer finally sent to investigate seemed to suggest that the abandonment of the child by the parent occurs more often than the general public might expect. But the officer had good news. Statistics, she said, indicate that in eighty percent of cases the absent parent returns to the child within six to twelve months. All we had to do was wait. We have heard nothing from the authorities since (except that the home address given by the girl had turned out to be a recently vacated house). We can only assume their silence indicates futility in the search for anyone who might care about this girl.

You Will Want to Be My Mother Again, For I Am Changed. The tang of soil soaked through with summertime rain fills my nostrils as I pull up a chair to deliver the bad news. No luck on her family, I say, but we continue to search. "My mother is coming," she tells herself. "It's my birthday soon. My mother would not miss my birthday. I'd like to arrange a special party. But I'll need your help."

The Birthday Party #1. Preparations will begin at first light. An orderly will prop open the doors to the ward and carry outside chairs and tables from the canteen. Arranged on the lawn they will await the guests. At least twenty rows of chairs will be required – ten chairs per row – for many people will be invited. "Friends and relatives," she says, when I ask who will be there. "And all the staff and patients at Longfield." If any patient is unable to walk, she explains, they will be pushed outside in their bed, and the beds will be arranged in a circle on the outer edge of the chairs, for no one must miss the party. The kind old oak will spread his canopy above the tables of food and keep the lemonade cool and stop the edges of the egg and cress sandwiches from turning to crust. The sky will be blue and sunlight will reflect off ice cubes. It might rain, I say. "It will be perfect. Sunny and warm with an occasional breeze." Dozens of balloons will be inflated. They will fly from poles to signal the location of the party. And if any guest cannot find their way, they need only follow the smiley-faced worms that will be crayoned on the walls and floor of the hospital corridors. They will be very excited, the party-goers. The invitation will describe the event as the best party to ever be thrown in honour of a birthday – for it is not a normal birthday, she points out, but a special birthday. She will not divulge in the invitation why it is special. That would spoil the surprise. In attendance at the party will be people from the life the girl had lived prior to Longfield. They will try not to stare at the new style of body she has come to inhabit. She will crawl and slide through the crowd, coil and twist around the feet of cousins and uncles. And when they ask where she vanished to, she will look up and say, from her small red mouth, "I had to go away. But I'm better now. Take a seat. And I'll show you."

The Birthday Party #2. We – the girl and I – must keep watch for her mother. "It is important the show begins only when my mother has arrived." She explains her mother will be seated with the other guests. And then, says the girl, she and I – the girl and the doctor – will take to the stage. It will be situated at the front of the crowd, constructed on a raised platform for an uncluttered view. The doctor, she says – and by this she means me – will present the show. He will introduce himself and welcome the audience. With his white coat and stethoscope and clever, eloquent speech he will command their respect. And onto the stage he will invite the magnificent worm-girl. She will flex her way over the ground, down the middle aisle toward the stage, using the front of her body the way she used to use legs, watched by everyone, elegantly inhuman in the afternoon light. During her journey to the stage the doctor will read from the picture book – the page entitled *W for Worm*. There are many interesting facts about worm-girl, he will tell the audience. Worm-girl, for example, can breathe underground. Worm-girl has reduced sight and hearing (her eyes and ears have partly closed) but – half-blind, half-deaf – she can detect light and vibration. She has five hearts, worm-girl, all in the lower half of her body. But she has no backbone, he explains. See how she displays the beauty of the invertebrate, he tells the audience, as she curls and uncurls – the equivalent for you or I, ladies and gentlemen, would be to touch the tip of your nose to the small of your back. Quite the sight! But now, he says, the most miraculous sight of all. Two nurses will lift worm-girl onto the stage and lay her down on a long table. The doctor will turn the page in the picture book. Fact number five, he will read aloud: if a worm finds itself sliced in half, it will become two worms. And the doctor will pick up a saw – the long type used for cutting wood – and rest its serrated teeth against worm-girl's waist, as she turns her head and scans the audience for the face of her mother.

The Birthday Party #3. One worm, the girl says, will contain her old heart – the faulty heart. That worm will perish, there and then on stage. The other worm, however, will sit up and smile, in good health. She shows me the picture in the book. In a two-panel illustration a bemused surgeon severs a worm but finds – lo and behold! – a pair of worms wriggling around on the operating table. What happens after I cut you in half, I ask. The audience, says the girl, will rise to its feet in rapturous applause. Her mother will run to the stage, crying and laughing. And although her new half-sized daughter will resemble a worm, her mother will look down at her face and see the face of her child. And she will hold her daughter proudly in the afternoon sun, remade, flawless and perfect.

ABOUT THE EDITORS

Allen Ashley is a British Fantasy Award winning editor and a prizewinning poet. He is the author or editor of fourteen published books including the novel *The Planet Suite* (Eibonvale Press, 2016) and the short story collection *Once and Future Cities* (Eibonvale Press, 2009). He works as a critical reader and also as a creative writing tutor with five groups currently running across north London, including the advanced science fiction and fantasy group, Clockhouse London Writers. He is a committee member for the British Fantasy Society. Website: www.allenashley.com

Sarah Doyle is Poet-in-Residence to the Pre-Raphaelite Society, for whom she writes commissioned new work, and co-judges an annual poetry competition. She is (with Allen Ashley) co-author of *Dreaming Spheres: Poems of the Solar System* (PS Publishing, 2014). Sarah has been a guest reader at numerous poetry venues; has been published widely in magazines, journals and anthologies; and placed in many competitions. She was Highly Commended in the Best Single Poem category of the Forward Prizes for Poetry 2018. Sarah holds a Creative Writing MA from Royal Holloway College, University of London, and works as a freelance manuscript critique provider. Website: www.sarahdoyle.co.uk

WRITERS' BIOGRAPHIES

Paul Stephenson was a winner in the 2014/2015 Poetry Business Book and Pamphlet competition. His resulting first pamphlet, *Those People*, was published in May 2015 by Smith/Doorstop. He has published two further pamphlets: *The Days that Followed Paris* (HappenStance 2016) and *Selfie with Waterlilies* (Paper Swans Press 2017). Paul has published poems in journals including *Magma*; *Poetry London*; *The Rialto*; *Bare Fiction*; and *The Interpreter's House*; and has reviewed for the *The North* and *PN Review*. He co-edited an issue of *Magma* on the theme of 'Europe', published in 2018. He has a blog at http://www.paulstep.com where he interviews poets.

Elaine Ewart lives in Ely and is currently studying for a PhD in Creative Writing at the University of Essex. Her poetry has been published in various anthologies and journals, including *Ariadne's Thread*; *The Fenland Reed*; *Dream Catcher*; and *Ink, Sweat and Tears*. In 2015 she was shortlisted for the Resurgence Ecopoetry Awards; and in 2012 she held the title of Fenland Poet Laureate.

Gary Budgen grew up and lives in London. His fiction has been published in many magazines and anthologies including *Where are we Going?* and *Sensorama* from Eibonvale. His collection, *Chrysalis*, is published by Horrified Press.

Sarah Westcott is a poet and writer living in Kent. Her debut pamphlet, *Inklings*, was a Poetry Book Society choice in 2013; and her first collection, *Slant Light*, was published by Pavilion Poetry and highly commended in the 2017 Forward Prizes. Recent awards include the London Magazine Poetry Prize and the Manchester Cathedral Poetry Prize. Her poems have been published on buses and beermats, and were installed in the trees at the Bethnal Green Nature Reserve in east London.

Cheryl Pearson lives and writes in Manchester in the North West of England. Her poems have appeared in publications including *The Guardian*; *Southword*; and *Frontier*; and she has twice been nominated for a Pushcart Prize. She also writes short and flash fiction, and was Highly Commended in the Costa Short Story Awards 2017. Her first full poetry collection, *Oysterlight*, is available now from Amazon/Pindrop Press.

Tarquin Landseer graduated from Royal Holloway, University of London with an MA in Creative Writing. He is a recipient of a Keats-Shelley Memorial Prize. In 2016 he won first prize in The International Welsh Poetry Competition. Various poems have appeared in *The Keats-Shelley Review*; *Staple*; *The Frogmore Papers*; *The Peloton Anthology* by Templar Poetry; and the anthology, *Bedford Square 10*.

Holly Heisey is an author, illustrator, and designer with a love of spaceships and a tendency to quote Monty Python. They've had stories in *Intergalactic Medicine Show*; *Escape Pod*; *Clockwork Phoenix 5*; and *Transcendent: The Year's Best Transgender Speculative Fiction volumes one and two*; as well as translated into German and Estonian. Holly is currently at work on a space opera epic, and you can find more of their fiction online at hollyheisey. com

Olivia Edwards has recently graduated from the University of Reading with a degree in Classical and Medieval Civilisation. Though a historian at heart, she has always loved writing both poetry and fiction. Now that she has finished university she has time to focus on creative writing again rather than just focus on essays. She has two dogs and a very angry cat. Her cat reviews all her work for her.

Scott Hughes's fiction, poetry, and essays have appeared in *Crazyhorse*; *One Sentence Poems*; *Entropy*; *Deep Magic*; *Carbon Culture Review*; *Redivider*; *Redheaded Stepchild*; *PopMatters*; *Strange Horizons*; *Chantwood Magazine*; *Odd Tales of Wonder*; *The Haunted Traveler*; *Exquisite Corpse*; *Pure Slush*; *Word Riot*; and *Compaso: Journal of Comparative Research in Anthropology and Sociology*. His fiction chapbook, *The Last Book You'll Ever Read*, is forthcoming from Weasel Press. For more information, visit writescott.com.

James Dorr's story, *Crow and Rat*, is set in the universe of his novel-in-stories, *Tombs: A Chronicle of Latter-Day Times of Earth*. Other books include *The Tears of Isis*, a 2013 Stoker Award® nominee for Superior Achievement in a Fiction Collection; *Strange Mistresses: Tales of Wonder and Romance*; *Darker Loves: Tales of Mystery and Regret*; and his all-poetry, *Vamps (A Retrospective)*. For the latest information, Indiana, USA resident Dorr invites readers to visit his blog at http://jamesdorrwriter.wordpress.com.

Kerry Darbishire is a songwriter turned poet who lives on a Cumbrian fellside. Since her mentorship with Judy Brown, poet in residence at the Wordsworth Trust in 2013, Kerry's poems have appeared in many anthologies and magazines. She has won several competitions and prizes, and was shortlisted in the Bridport Prize 2017. Her first poetry collection, *A Lift of Wings*, was published in 2014 by Indigo Dreams. Her second, *Distance Sweet on my Tongue*, is to be published in Autumn 2018.

Jonathan Edwards's first collection of poems, *My Family and Other Superheroes* (Seren), received the Costa Poetry Award and the Wales Book of the Year People's Choice Award. It was shortlisted for the Fenton Aldeburgh First Collection Prize.

Tonya Walter lives in Minnesota with two children and a husband. After realizing that heavily redacted resumés don't fare well in the job market, she walked away from a burgeoning career as a ghost-writer to work odd jobs (the oddest she can find) and write disturbing stories about carnivorous plants and haunted airplanes. Strange bits of her fiction and weird art can be found at thefictitioustonyawalter.com

Lauren Mason is a musician and nurse from London. She has an MA in Poetry from Newcastle University/The Poetry School, graduating in 2018. Her poems have been published in places including *The Interpreter's House*; *Brittle Star*; and *Hotdog*.

Setareh Ebrahimi is a poet and writer living and working in Faversham, Kent. She completed her Bachelor's in English Literature from The University of Westminster in 2014, and her Master's in English and American Literature from The University of Kent in 2016. She has been published numerous times in various journals and magazines, including *Brittle Star*; *Thanet Poetry Journal*; and *Dissonance*. Setareh has just released her first pamphlet of poetry, entitled *In My Arms*, from Bad Betty Press. She performs regularly at different events in Kent and London, as well as hosting her own poetry and culture evenings.

Ian Steadman is a writer from the south of England. His stories have most recently been published in *Black Static*; *Unsung Stories*; *The Lonely Crowd*; *STORGY*; *Coffin Bell*; *Night-Light* (Midnight Street anthology); and *The Year's Best Body Horror*. You can find him at www.iansteadman.com, or he occasionally manifests on Twitter as @steadmanfiction

Kate Wise has been published in various magazines in print and online, including *The Rialto*; *Poems in Which*; and *Structo*. Translations/reworkings of Sappho and Catullus have also been published, most recently by Sidekick Books. Her poem on Urinal Blocks was a winner in the *Poetry News* Members' Poems competition, and she appeared in Eyewear's *Best New British* *and Irish Poets 2017*. Her work (both for adults and children) has appeared in several anthologies by The Emma Press, with a further two upcoming in 2018. She grew up in Cheshire, lives in London, and tweets at @kwise62.

Frank Roger was born in 1957 in Ghent, Belgium. His first story appeared in 1975. Since then his stories appear in an increasing number of languages in all sorts of magazines and anthologies, and since 2000, story collections are published, also in various languages. Apart from fiction, he also produces collages and graphic work in a surrealist and satirical tradition. They have appeared in various magazines and books. By now he has a few hundred short stories to his credit, published in more than forty languages. Find out more at www. frankroger.be

Jayne Stanton lives in Leicestershire. Her poems have appeared in numerous print and online magazines, and anthologies including *Best British and Irish Poets 2017* (Eyewear) and *DIVERSIFLY* (Fair Acre Press). She has written commissions for a county museum; University of Leicester's Centre for New Writing; UoL poems for International Women's Day 2018; and a city residency. A pamphlet, *Beyond the Tune*, is published by Soundswrite Press (2014).

William Stephenson's first full collection, *Travellers and Avatars*, will be published by Live Canon in 2018. His pamphlets are *Rain Dancers in the Data Cloud* (Templar, 2012); and *Source Code* (Ravenglass, 2013), downloadable at: http://chesterrep. openrepository.com/cdr/bitstream/10034/336895/11/Stephenson-source+code.pdf

Sandra Unerman is a retired Government lawyer who lives in London. Her fantasy novels, *Spellhaven* and *Ghosts and Exiles*, are published by Mirror World. She writes reviews and articles for the British Science Fiction Association and for the British Fantasy Society. She is a member of Clockhouse London Writers and her interests include folklore and history.

Megan Pattie lives on the north east coast of England. She was a Foyle Young Poet of the Year in 2009, and since then her work has appeared in a variety of online and print publications, including *Ink, Sweat and Tears*; *The Black Light Engine Room*; and *The Emma Press Anthology of the Sea*.

Kristin Camitta Zimet is the author of *Take in My Arms the Dark* (a full-length collection of poetry) and the editor of *The Sow's Ear Poetry Review*. Her poems are in over 100 journals and anthologies in the United States and the United Kingdom, lately including *Salamander*; *Crannog*; and *Natural Bridge*. She also works as a Master Naturalist, running bird counts; and she is a Reiki master, treating both animals and humans.

Self-proclaimed 'Glasgow Surrealist' **Douglas Thompson** has authored thirteen books since 2009, ranging from novels to short story and poetry collections, variously classed as Slipstream, Sci-Fi, Horror, Literary and Historical Fiction. His website is: www. douglasthompson.wordpress.com/

Amanda Oosthuizen's stories and poems have been published online, in print, in galleries, in Winchester Cathedral and pasted up on the London Underground. Recent successes include the Winchester Poetry Prize and The Pre-Raphaelite Society Poetry Prize. Work is forthcoming in *Riggwelter*; *Prelude*; *Lonesome October Lit*; and *Ambit*. Amanda has an MA with Distinction in Creative Writing from the University of Chichester, where she was joint winner of the Kate Betts Prize. She earns her living by writing and arranging music and teaching woodwind.

Lindsay Reid is a poet living in Newcastle upon Tyne. She received a PhD in Creative Writing from Newcastle University in 2016 and her first poetry collection is due to be published shortly by Red Squirrel Press. She has had poems published in *Magma*; *Mslexia*; and *The Cadaverine*; and has won several poetry competitions.

Elaine Ruth White writes for page, stage and broadcast, with past work including commissions from English Touring Opera and the BBC as well as theatre companies. Her first short story has just been published in *Cornish Short Stories: A Collection of Contemporary Short Stories*. She was the editor of an illustrated poetry anthology, *Coasters*, with Atlantic Press and also writes non-fiction as Elaine Farrell.

David Hartley has written many strange tales about animals, some of which have appeared in print. There is one about an elephant in *Ambit*; one about a fox in *Structo*; and a particularly unsettling one about a pig in *Black Static*, among many others. One day, the whole menagerie may well be brought together in a full collection. Until then, Hartley is working on a Creative Writing PhD at The University of Manchester and can be found haunting the spoken word scene of the North West. He tweets: @DHartleyWriter, and lives with one human, two rabbits and nine guinea pigs.

Diana Cant is a child and adolescent psychotherapist who has spent almost all her working life in the field of mental health. She has more recently begun to focus on communicating about the lives of children in a poetic rather than a clinical form, and is a student on the Poetry School MA course. She lives and works in Kent.

Mary Livingstone is a sustainability consultant from Manchester. Her poems have been published in various places, including *Lighthouse* and *Poetry News*, and have been placed in competitions. As well as writing poetry, she co-edits the literary magazine, *The Fenland Reed*: www.thefenlandreed.co.uk / @TheFenlandReed.

Bindia Persaud was born in Georgetown, Guyana, grew up in the north of England, and now resides in Ontario, Canada. Her work has appeared in *Zetetic: a Record of Unusual Inquiry*; *Kaaterskill Basin Literary Journal*; *Gone Lawn*; the *Bloody Key Society Periodical*; and the *Colored Lens*.

Michael G. Casey has published five books and numerous poems and short stories. Six of his plays have been performed. He holds a PhD from Cambridge University.

Jane Burn is a North East based artist and writer. Her poems have been featured in magazines such as *The Rialto*; *Under the Radar*; *Butcher's Dog*; *Iota Poetry*, and many more; as well as anthologies from the Emma Press, Beautiful Dragons, Seren, Emergency Poet, and Kind of a Hurricane Press. Her pamphlets include *Fat Around the Middle*, published by Talking Pen; and *Tongues of Fire*, published by the BLER Press. Her first full collection, *nothing more to it than bubbles*, has been published by Indigo Dreams. She has had four poems longlisted in the National Poetry Competition from 2014 to 2017; was commended and highly commended in the Yorkmix Poetry Competition 2014 and 2015; won the inaugural Northern Writes Poetry Competition in 2017; and came second in the 2017 Welsh International Poetry Competition.

Jane Lovell has been widely published in journals and anthologies. She won the Flambard Prize in 2015 and has been shortlisted for the Basil Bunting Prize, the Alpine Fellowship Writing Prize and the Wisehouse International Poetry Prize. Her recently published pamphlets are *Metastatic* by Against the Grain Poetry Press; *One Tree* by Night River Wood; and the prize-winning *Forbidden* by Coast to Coast to Coast. Her website is at https://janelovell128. wixsite.com/janelovellpoetry

Tracey Emerson's short stories have been widely published in anthologies and literary magazines. She has a PhD in Creative Writing from The University of Edinburgh and works as a literary consultant and writing tutor. Her debut thriller, *She Chose Me*, will be published by Legend Press in October 2018. You can find out more about Tracey and enjoy some of her short stories at: www. traceyemerson.com

Jenny Grassl was raised in Collegeville, Pennsylvania, and now lives in Cambridge, Massachusetts. Her poems have appeared or are forthcoming in various journals, including *Radar Poetry*; *Clarion*; *LIT*; *Ocean State Review*; and *Rogue Agent*.

Hannah Linden, with Gram Joel Davies, won the Cheltenham Festival Compound Poetry Competition 2015. She was Highly Commended in the Prole Laureate Competition 2015, and was longlisted for The Rialto Nature Poetry Competition 2018. Her poetry has been published in varied magazines and anthologies, most recently with *And Other Poems*; *Ink, Sweat and Tears*; *Amaryllis*; and *The Interpreter's House*; and is upcoming in *Magma*; *Lighthouse*; and *Domestic Cherry*. She is working towards her first collection, *Wolf Daughter*, which explores the impact of parental suicide. Twitter @hannahl1n

Ian Kappos is the author of a chapbook of fiction, *Crossfaded in Narnia* (Eibonvale Press, 2018). His Pushcart Prize-nominated writing has appeared in numerous magazines and anthologies. Co-editor of *Milkfist* and former editorial assistant at *Sublevel*, he also plays in the hardcore punk band, Cross Class. Though originally from Northern California, he currently lives in Los Angeles where he is an MFA candidate at CalArts. Find him online at www.iankappos.net, or on Twitter @Kappos_Ian.

Jason Gould is a Creative Writing graduate from the University of Hull. His short crime story, *Not the '60s Anymore*, was published in *Bloody Hull* (Mulholland Books / Hodder) after winning joint first prize in the Dead Pretty City crime writing competition, part of the literary celebrations for Hull UK City of Culture 2017. Other stories have been published in *Terror Tales of Yorkshire* (Gray Friar Press); *Structo*; *Beneath the Ground* (Alchemy Press); *Neon Lit: The Time Out Book of New Writing Vol 1*; *Crimewave*; *The Third Alternative*; and *Black Static*.